Macroproject Development
in the Third World

Westview Replica Editions

The concept of Westview Replica Editions is a response to the continuing crisis in academic and informational publishing. Library budgets for books have been severely curtailed. Ever larger portions of general library budgets are being diverted from the purchase of books and used for data banks, computers, micromedia, and other methods of information retrieval. Interlibrary loan structures further reduce the edition sizes required to satisfy the needs of the scholarly community. Economic pressures (particularly inflation and high interest rates) on the university presses and the few private scholarly publishing companies have severely limited the capacity of the industry to properly serve the academic and research communities. As a result, many manuscripts dealing with important subjects, often representing the highest level of scholarship, are no longer economically viable publishing projects --or, if accepted for publication, are typically subject to lead times ranging from one to three years.

Westview Replica Editions are our practical solution to the problem. We accept a manuscript in camera-ready form, typed according to our specifications, and move it immediately into the production process. As always, the selection criteria include the importance of the subject, the work's contribution to scholarship, and its insight, originality of thought, and excellence of exposition. The responsibility for editing and proofreading lies with the author or sponsoring institution. We prepare chapter headings and display pages, file for copyright, and obtain Library of Congress Cataloging in Publication Data. A detailed manual contains simple instructions for preparing the final typescript, and our editorial staff is always available to answer questions.

The end result is a book printed on acid-free paper and bound in sturdy library-quality softcovers. We manufacture these books ourselves using equipment that does not require a lengthy make-ready process and that allows us to publish first editions of 300 to 600 copies and to reprint even smaller quantities as needed. Thus, we can produce Replica Editions quickly and can keep even very specialized books in print as long as there is a demand for them.

About the Book and Author

Macroproject Development in the Third World:
An Analysis of Transnational Partnerships
Kathleen J. Murphy

During the 1970s an unprecedented number of large-scale projects of various kinds were launched in the Third World. Many multinational corporations that were experienced in initiating such projects in industrialized nations encountered unanticipated difficulties and risks in the new settings. This book assesses the experiences of multinationals and host nations and offers guidelines for effectively implementing macroprojects in developing areas.

The author synthesizes data from more than 1600 macroprojects conducted during the 1970s; statistical information was supplemented by on-site surveys and interviews. She emphasizes that the successful development of a large-scale project hinges on the effective coordination of numerous individuals and groups—owners, project management contractors, indigeneous and foreign workers, financiers, government ministeries, consumers, etc. The key to success, she concludes, lies in anticipating and managing for sociocultural discontinuities and in setting up an adequate audit of organizational effectiveness. The guidelines resulting from her analysis are intended to assist multinational corporations and their host counterparts in understanding the new arrangements and approaches needed to successfully manage the macroprojects of the future.

Ms. Murphy is an independent consultant based in New York City. Research for this book was conducted while she was a research consultant for McKinsey and Company, an international management consulting firm.

Macroproject Development in the Third World

An Analysis of Transnational Partnerships

Kathleen J. Murphy

Westview Press / Boulder, Colorado

A Westview Replica Edition

Copyright © 1983 by Westview Press, Inc.

Published in 1983 in the United States of America by
    Westview Press, Inc.
    5500 Central Avenue
    Boulder, Colorado 80301
    Frederick A. Praeger, President and Publisher

Library of Congress Cataloging in Publication Data
Murphy, Kathleen J.
Macroproject development in the third world.
    (A Westview Replica Edition)
    Index: p. 185
    1. Industrial project management. 2. Economic development projects.
3. Underdeveloped areas--International business enterprises. I. Title.
II. Series.
HD69.P75M87 1982   658.4'04'091724   82-19998
ISBN 0-86531-935-9

Printed and bound in the United States of America.

10 9 8 7 6 5 4 3 2 1

"The age of nations is past. The task before us now, if we would not perish, is to shake off our ancient prejudices, and to build the earth."

— Teilhard de Chardin

"There is no going backwards, but in the very moment of deepest need (there is) a hitherto undreamt-of movement forwards and outwards."

— Martin Buber

===

Dedication

To all the individuals — the owners, the project managers, the indigenous and foreign workers and professionals, local citizenry, international financiers, buyers of the output, government officials, etc. — who ushered these worldscale "grand pyramids of the 1970s" into existence. Working on a daily basis at the cutting edge of "progress" it was within the scope of their daily responsibilities to push for breakthroughs and insights in management, technology, socio-cultural evolution, etc. Joining these projects from diverse social, cultural, economic and educational backgrounds, heritages and experiences, the more than 10,000 people per project required to bring a typical worldscale achievement to fruition provided a source of strength as well as enhanced the complexity of these macroprojects.

Something beyond the easy, the convenient, the traditional drove these people to undertake these "macro" commitments. As one journalist remarked of the official dedication of a macroproject installation: "The dedication was there long before the ceremony."

Contents

List of Tables and Figures

Tables

xii

Figures

Preface

The decade of the 1970s saw an enormous step forward in investment activity throughout the developing world. The oil crisis of 1973 enabled Third World governments to indulge their spirit of nationalism by launching industrial and infrastructural projects on a scale comparable to the industrialized West. The magnitude of effort that has been invested in macroproject development (any project over $100 million) throughout the Third World from 1970 to 1979 is the focus of this book. Developing countries have been mounting these development projects on a scale that is awesome by any measure. Between 1970 and 1979, well over 900 macroprojects were begun, representing a total investment of over $500 billion. At least another 600 macroprojects are on the drawing boards. If all are brought to fruition, the investments will total more than $1 trillion. Fueled primarily by the shift in power and financial resources created by the oil crisis, project activity is going on not only, as might be expected, in resource development, but in processing industries such as metal refining, smelting, and petro-chemicals, and also in infrastructure, including the burgeoning of whole cities and industrial parks, massive desalination plants, roadways, and ports.

Developing countries were not able to implement projects of such magnitude entirely on their own, however. They depended on multinational corporations to provide the capital, technology, man-agement and market access which — in many cases — they lacked. The efforts at transnational and transcorporate collaboration which

xvi

resulted did not always go smoothly. Multinationals with considerable experience in similar projects in an industrialized environment found that they had great difficulties in the Third World.
Though their commitment to budget and schedule obligations was
sincere, the enormous gap in social and cultural values and modes of
operation, as well as the number of stakeholders involved often
threw the projects out of control.

A major feature of the decade of the 1970s was an expansion
in the range of postures developing countries and multinationals
adopted toward each other. Certainly, developing countries were
taking increasingly firm attitudes about their rights to project
ownership and profits. For this, they had the model of nationalizations that occurred as an aftermath of the oil crisis, as well as
the independence that the gush of oil dollars brought to oil-
producing countries. Multinationals, although often stripped of
ownership of supply sources, entered into numerous arrangements to
continue some measure of managerial control and continuity of
supply.

The notion that ownership and control are synonymous is no
longer true. The relationship between risks, ownership, and control
has been freed to be set in a balance appropriate both to the
complexity of particular projects and the varying contributions of
the principal parties. Many new contractual alternatives and
combinations have been developed over the last decade as a result
of these trends.

This newly enlarged field of alternatives for establishing
partnerships argues for new perspectives on the parties concerned.
For the purposes of this book, an extension of the "host country"
metaphor (commonly used to designate the developing country in
which macroprojects are initiated) is proposed. Participants from
developing countries will be referred to as "host" participants; the
multinationals as "guest" participants. Implied in this idea is a
reciprocity and flexibility in defining the responsibilities and
expectations for the relationship. Within this context, the hosts are
expected to provide a stable environment for the duration of the
project by interfacing with local governments and communities, and
by strictly adhering to the contractual agreement. The guest
multinationals, on the other hand, bearing their gifts of technology,
capital, or access to global markets, are expected to offer these

efficiently and effectively with due regard and respect for the local situation and indigenous capabilities.

This new perspective is extremely important, as a key aspect of macroprojects is the human side of transnational collaboration and the amount of attention that it demands. One of the more important human factors is the need for effective project leadership to establish and preserve the economic integrity of a macroproject. The responsibilities and tasks of the various participants need to be coordinated and directed. An organizational approach must be designed to bridge the gap between the multinational guests and their Third World counterparts.

The analysis of transnational partnerships that follows is based on a massive data collection effort sponsored by McKinsey & Company, Inc. Chiefly through the analysis of published material, more than 1600 projects of $100 million or more were tracked from January 1970 through June 1979 in 90 of 120 developing countries. Later, the scope of the study was expanded to include Australia and New Zealand. (Like many developing nations, both of these countries require extensive financial, technological, and marketing help from foreign enterprises in order to exploit their untapped resources.) For each macroproject, a project history was compiled that included data on participating companies, type of involvement, project scope, and changes in costs and completion dates. To check and amplify the statistical findings, a field survey was conducted in Southeast Asia, Oceania, and Latin America. It should be noted that because this is a statistical study the following analysis presents a global perspective. Thus, the reader should be aware that certain important issues may not be addressed at the level of depth they deserve because of the limits of the survey research approach.

Acknowledgements

I am very grateful to all the multinational and host companies, client organizations, and government officials, representative of the macroproject sample of participants, whom I have interviewed over the past several years as part of the research for this book. Their comments, insights, accessibility and courtesy are deeply appreciated.

I would also like to acknowledge the support of several people at McKinsey & Company, Inc., without whom the research project might never have reached fruition. Ken Ohmae (Tokyo), and Roger Abravanel (Milan) actively promoted my research within the Firm and among their clients, thus making it possible for me to update the database and advance the research methodology. Melanie McArthur (New York) was involved at the very early stages of the macroproject database construction, and she has provided encouragement, solid judgement and important insights which have been invaluable to me over the past seven years.

The figures and tables in this book are being reproduced with the permission of McKinsey & Company, Inc.

My parents, brothers and sisters, and all my very special friends have been very patient and supportive during the many years of intensive research on this subject.

More immediately, I have enjoyed the encouragement and enthusiasm of Frank Davidson of the Macro-Engineering Research Group at M.I.T. who very much shares my interests and commitment to macro-engineering. I am also very grateful to Jonathon Aronson and Daniel Bradford who encouraged me to undertake this book. Of course, this work would never be realized without the lively interest xx

and assistance of Fred Praeger, Dean Birkenkamp, Michael Rosenberg, and Kathy Wilson of Westview Press.

Finally, I am enormously indebted to the small cadre on the scenes during the preparation of this book who made important contributions to the quality of the final product: Patricia Sherman made valuable comments and suggestions on the manuscript; and Sam Chapin of "Typing With A Memory" did an excellent job in coordinating the preparation of the camera-ready typescript by wordprocessor.

1
The Need for
Close Collaboration

> Companhia Vale do Rio Doce (CVRD) plans to
> build, in collaboration with a consortium of Ja-
> panese firms, an aluminum smelter and an alumi-
> num refinery complex near Belem (Brazil) with an
> ultimate capacity of 640,000 metric tons per year,
> a level not reached by any existing plant in the
> world.*

...Announcements of this kind were becoming more and more
frequent throughout the 1970s, with one year's record-breaking
project following hard on the heels and eclipsing the fame of the
previous year's record-breaking project. The impetus for mounting
these projects of unprecedented size arose from the desire of newly
oil-rich countries to undertake massive industrial development, as
well as the necessity, faced by most Third World countries, of
expanding the scope of their primary projects to include extensive
infrastructure support.

The Belem project, described in the press release cited above,
is a good example of the sometimes erratic fortunes of these vast
projects which require enormous concentrations of resources and
effort — yet provide little assurance of success. A joint venture
between CVRD and Nippon Amazon Aluminum Company of Tokyo, a
Japanese consortium of 32 firms, the Belem project was originally
slated to cost $2.5 billion. When costs escalated to $3.3 billion, the
project was considerably scaled down before being abandoned in
1977. Later revived at the scaled down level, the project was
subsequently projected to cost $4 billion to $5 billion. This example
of the way in which project histories become erratic even before

*Japan Chemical, December 4, 1975. Emphasis added.

they get under way, suggests that conventional notions of when to proceed with a project, when to abandon it, what is economically sound and strategically advantageous may be inadequate for understanding the macroproject arena in developing countries today.

An overview of the distinguishing features of these projects is necessary in order to appreciate the contributions and achievements of participants in these macroprojects and the difficulties they face. It is the unique challenges of macroproject development that create the enormous and pressing need for close collaboration among all who are directly or indirectly involved. This chapter describes how the macroprojects under consideration are:

- The largest undertakings known to date
- Beyond the capabilities of any single organization
- Difficult to control
- Socially and culturally incongruous

LARGEST UNDERTAKINGS KNOWN TO DATE

On a worldwide basis, projects over $100 million are frequently referred to as "worldscale" projects. Particularly within the context of developing countries, projects over $100 million tower above all other enterprises by virtue of the investment they represent for the country, and their impact on the local economy. Whether a $100 million mine in West Africa or a $5 billion liquified natural gas processing plant in the Middle East, the projects challenge the capabilities and strain the resources of developing nations. Within such country settings, individual undertakings over $100 million investment loom large — large enough to be designated macroprojects. Although they exhibit characteristics that are found in projects outside the developing world, as will be discussed, these characteristics are intensified because of the settings in which the projects unfold. However, the rewards of participation — whether as equity holder or contractor — are attractive enough to draw many companies into the macroproject arena. In the macroprojects under discussion, over 3,000 companies are active in providing equity, loans, capital goods and engineering services in the Third World.

In undertaking macroprojects in developing countries, the participants assume enormous responsibilities, as these macroprojects are highly complex in scope, extremely challenging to implement, and take place in countries whose resources are already

extremely burdened by other macroprojects simultaneously underway. These projects tax the limits of existing technologies,
managerial capabilities and local support facilities.

Individually Highly Complex in Scope

Today's macroprojects in the developing world are concerned
both with installing basic resource extraction and processing
industries, as well as with an infrastructure of supporting services
(power, transport, communications, and public or social facilities)
(Figure 1.1) Looking at projects from the standpoint of percent of
total investment, one can see that hydrocarbon processing accounts
for 23 percent of the total; metals, 18 percent; other industry, 6
percent and infrastructure 47 percent. The average project costs
roughly $500 million.

These projects increase in scope as they increase in investment. At the lower cost levels, one can find simple installations —
e.g., cement plants, pulp and paper mills — that seldom require
additional infrastructure to develop; in fact, they often follow after
the basic infrastructure has been installed. At the higher cost levels
enormously complex resource and infrastructure projects can be
found: If a resource project is located in an undeveloped area
(which is often the case), it cannot even be started until roads and
other infrastructural improvements or installations have been made.
Often the complexity of such a project is compounded by the
intricate engineering or technological requirements associated with
it. Thus, the largest projects include infrastructural components.
On the other hand, if an infrastructure project entails building
roadways, installing power plants and communications networks, and
the like, that is nationwide or even regional in scope, it can be more
costly and more complex than the resource project with infrastructural components.

To demonstrate the interplay between resource development
and infrastructural components within a macroproject's scope, the
Al Jubail Industrial City, the Bandar Abbas Steel Complex, and the
Asahan Aluminum Smelter projects are described below.

- The Al Jubail Industrial City currently underway in Saudi
  Arabia includes three petrochemical plants, an oil refinery,
  steel and aluminum plants, water and waste treatment
  facilities, a desalination plant, housing, a training center, a

Figure 1.1

Summary of Macroprojects by Industry/Infrastructure Element
January 1970 through June 1979

		Number Of Projects	Average Value Per Project ($ Millions)	Total Value Of Projects ($ Billions)	Percentage Of Total Value
Hydrocarbon Processing Industry	Fuel (Refinery, LNG, Gas)	170	$ 554	$ 95.2	9.4%
	Pipelines	62	881	54.6	5.4
	Petrochemical/Chemical	113	516	58.3	5.8
	Fertilizer	110	250	27.5	2.7
	Total	460	$ 512	$235.6	23.3%
Metal (Mining, Smelting, Refining) Industry *	Steel	105	$ 909	$ 95.4	9.4%
	Aluminum	85	382	32.5	3.2
	Copper	67	354	23.7	2.3
	Nickel	29	322	9.3	0.9
	Other Metals	31	638	19.8	2.0
	Total	317	$ 570	$180.7	17.8%
Other Industry *	Chemical Minerals	31	$ 283	$ 8.8	0.9%
	Cement	28	168	4.7	0.5
	Pulp and Paper	72	252	18.1	1.8
	Manufacturing	48	576	27.6	2.7
	Total	179	$ 331	$ 59.2	5.9%
	Subtotal Industries	956	$ 497	$475.5	47.0%
Infra-Structure**	Power	219	$ 658	$144.2	14.3%
	Transport	199	798	158.7	15.7
	Communications	27	1,939	52.3	5.2
	Social Facilities	186	573	106.6	10.5
	Government Facilities	17	777	13.2	1.3
	Subtotal Infrastructure	648	$ 733	$475.0	47.0%
	Industrial Cities*	10	$6,036	$ 60.4	6.0%
Total Projects		1,614	$ 626	$1,010.9	100.0%

*Includes infrastructure when part of project scope.
**Includes projects designed solely to install or improve infrastructure.
***Excludes industrial plants where possible.

seaport, and an international airport. The original cost projection of $9 billion in 1975 has already swollen to $20 billion. An impressive undertaking by any stretch of the imagination, this project undoubtedly represents one of the most difficult coordination and management challenges to date. (Upon close examination, one can see that it is a collage of multiple medium-scale macroprojects — that is, a single petrochemical plant, oil refinery, or airport would, in itself, comprise a macroproject of more than $100 million.)

- The Bandar Abbas Steel Complex in Iran, expected to cost $3.6 billion, was designed to produce three million tons-per-year. Originally it included a railroad, a six-lane highway, a 500-megawatt power plant, a natural gas line and a new city with a capacity of 800,000 people. Suffering from a cost escalation of 80 percent in the first year, the project had to be scaled down in a number of ways, particularly by abandoning plans for the city. Eventually, this project was one of many brought to a grinding halt in February 1979, when the Shah was deposed.

- The Asahan Aluminum Smelter project in Indonesia, a $1.8 billion investment, has a construction program that includes a 225,000 ton-per-year smelter in North Sumatra, and a 513-megawatt power plant on the Asahan River. Other aspects of this project include port facilities (including pier, berth, loading facilities) and roads (both temporary and access roads for the smelter site, and several new roads and improvements to existing roads for the power site). A permanent operators' camp including administrative offices, housing, schools, churches, mosques, hospitals, sports grounds, and markets is being built to serve the smelter site. The project will also provide telecommunications and water facilities.

In contrast, the smaller projects appear much more straightforward: The $160 million thermal power and desalination plant in Dabaya, Abu Dhabi has some infrastructural requirements — but nowhere near the scale of the three projects just described. The $167 million fertilizer plant in Panipat, India is a "plant-export" type facility consisting of a 900 tons-per-day ammonia and a 1,500 tons-per-day urea unit.

The need for industrial and infrastructure advances was so acute in the 1970s that only macroprojects seemed to provide sufficient impetus for growth. The top twenty macroprojects include extremely ambitious infrastructure projects, as well as industrial development projects with extensive infrastructural requirements (Table 1.1). There are several notable features of these

Table 1.1

Top Twenty Macroprojects

	Project Name	Location	Curr. Invest- ment ($ Bill.)	Curr. Compl. Date	Stage	Owners	Lead Project Managers
1	Saudi Arabia Gas- Processing, Pipeline	Saudi Arabia	21.0	1985	Contract let	Aramco	Fluor
2	Telecommunications System – Phase 1	Egypt	20.0	1983	RFP	Areto	Con. Telephone Co. Gen. Tel & Elec.
3	Al Jubail Industrial City	Saudi Arabia	20.0	1997	Underway	Sabic	Bechtel
4	ChungChong-Namdoyor Kyongsanbuk–Tu Steel	South Korea	15.0		RFP	Pohang Iron & Steel Co.	
5	Contrywide Telecomm. Network	Iran	15.0	1988	Suspended	Telecom. Co. of Iran	American Bell Int'l.
6	Trans–Turkey Highway	Turkey	14.0		Plan	Turkey Government	Spec.
7	Iraq Telephone System	Iraq	10.0		Plan	Iraq Government	
8	Sepetiba Uranium Oxide Plant	Brazil	10.0	1978	Contract let	Nuclebras	
9	Zulia Steel Complex	Venezuela	10.0	1990	Negotiations	Corpozulia Davy Ashmore Int'l Complejo Sider De Zulia	British Steel
10	South of Riyadh New City	SaudiArabia	10.0	1983	Plan	S. Arabia Government	

#	Project	Country	Value	Year	Status	Owner	Contractor
11	Yanbu Industrial Project	Saudi Arabia	10.0	2006	Contract let	Sabic	Parsons, Ralph M. / Fluor
12	Ruweis Industrial Centre Infrastructure	Abu Dhabi	10.0	1992	Contract let	Abu Dhabi Natl. Oil	Fluor
13	Itaipu Hydro Power/Dam	Brazil	9.0	1988	Construction	Itaipu Binacional / Electrobras / Ande	CIEM (Brazil)** / Int'l. Engineering* / Electroconsult*
14	Las Truchas Steel Mill	Mexico	8.0	1994	Construction	Sid Laz Carden / Las Truchas / Mexican Government / Altos Hornos De Mexico / Min. of National Properties Nafinsa	
15	King Khalid Military City	Saudi Arabia	7.0	1985	Contract let	Moda	US Army Corps Eng. / Morrison, Knudsen
16	Road Pavement	Saudi Arabia	7.0		Agreed	S. Arabia Gov't	Korea Hghwy. Corp.
17	Bushehr Nuclear/Desal	Iran	6.9	1981	Abandoned	Atomic Energy Org.	Kraftwerk Union / Sasakura Eng.
18	Federal Capital New City	Nigeria	6.0	1997	Contract let	Nigerian Fed. Cap. Dev. Auth.	IPA
19	KRA Isthmus Canal	Thailand	6.0		Talks stop	Thai Oil Co.	
20	Esfahan Nuclear Power (2)	Iran	5.0	1984	Talks stop	Iran Atomic Energy Auth	Kraftwerk Union

* – Consulting or design only.
** – Construction only, or turnkey contracts that include design.

largest projects: First of all, these largest projects are sponsored mostly by government ministeries or parastatal corporations (or state enterprises) from the host country. Overall, a disproportionate number are nationwide infrastructure development projects — telecommunications, power, highway systems, canals, new cities — projects which tax the public sectors of these countries, such as their government ministeries, and public financing capabilities. Secondly, twenty percent of these top projects have been suspended or abandoned. These have been kept on the list of top twenty, nevertheless, as revivals are not uncommon for projects at this level of complexity. Once technological, financial, or other problems are resolved, or once demand increases, feasibility studies might be dusted off, and discussions might be initiated again. Third, these worldscale projects are managed by the industry leaders — more than half of the lead project managers (on the projects with contracts let) are from the United States. These companies are known for their project management capabilities (Fluor, Bechtel, Parsons), their technology (Continental Telephone, GTE, American Bell International), as well as their engineering and design capabilities (International Engineering, U.S. Army Corps of Engineers). However, the award of a $7 billion road pavement job by Saudi Arabia to the Korea Highway Corporation should be noted as an important indication of the advancements being made by host locals in the international arena. The fact that a Korean company was awarded lead responsibility for management of a multi-billion dollar project outside its home country is a sign of the development that Third World corporations have individually achieved over the last decade. (This will be discussed in Chapter 2.) In general, players who could manage such enormous complexity have been in high demand.

Collectively An Extensive Development Portfolio

In addition to the complexity involved in marshalling a single project from planning through design, engineering, construction and start-up, it should be noted that these developing countries as a whole are shouldering an enormous development commitment — whether measured by number of projects, or geographic concentration. Viewed over the last decade, the projects have been steadily increasing in number and size. Figure 1.2 shows the

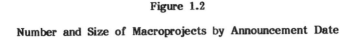

Figure 1.2

Number and Size of Macroprojects by Announcement Date

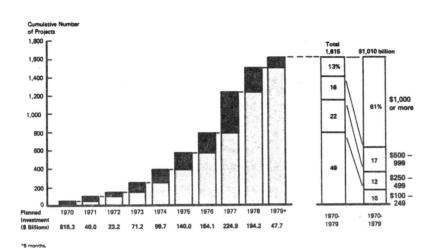

acceleration of project announcements between January 1970 and June 1979. The numbers of projects currently planned or underway have increased more than thirtyfold, ranging in size from $100 million to over $1 billion, and representing an investment of more than $1 trillion. The mix by size has remained constant year by year over the 10-year period. Of special note is the timing of the announcements: Over 85 percent of the 1,615 projects (86 percent of the total investment) were announced in the period following the oil crisis; 1977 being the record year, with roughly 25 percent of the 10-year totals having been announced in that year.

The immediate impact of this macroproject activity on global industry supply/demand balances may not be as dramatic as the large number of projects listed for most industry sectors might seem to suggest, for the long lifecycles of projects and their diverse startup dates extend the planned completion over many years.

Scanning the developing world as a whole, macroprojects are spread throughout 90 of the 120 developing nations. An example of the distribution of projects and investment by geographic region shows that 13 percent of the developing nations (the 18 countries in the Middle East and North Africa) account for more than two-fifths of the investment (Figure 1.3). This suggests that the resource

Figure 1.3

Distribution of Projects by Geographic Region
January 1970 through June 1979

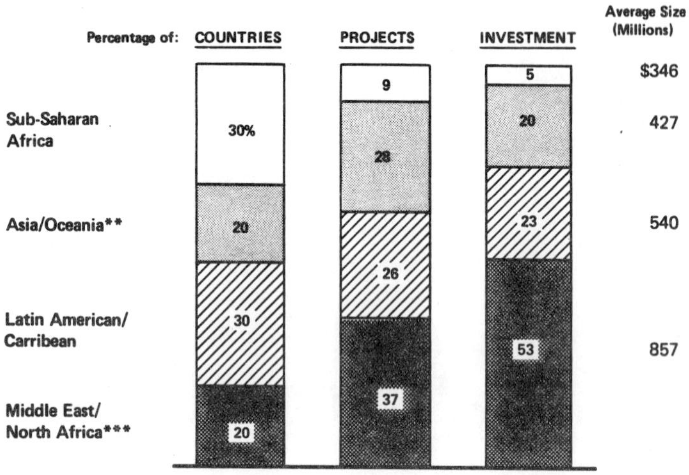

Distribution of Projects by Geographic Region chart showing Percentage of: COUNTRIES, PROJECTS, INVESTMENT, and Average Size (Millions).

	COUNTRIES	PROJECTS	INVESTMENT	Average Size (Millions)
Sub-Saharan Africa	30%	9 / 28	5 / 20	$346 / 427
Asia/Oceania**	20	26	23	540
Latin American/ Carribean	30	37	53	857
Middle East/ North Africa***	20			

*Excluding South Africa

**Australia and New Zealand, Non - Third-World countries have been included for comparative purposes

***Excluding Israel

richness of a country and the level of its development affect investment size. Thus, the most expensive projects are found in OPEC countries, where there is a concentration of capital, a wealth of resources, and a need to develop local infrastructure. Although the need for infrastructure may be equally great in the Southwestern and Western parts of Africa, countries there have fewer resources and less capital available to justify the launching of numerous macroprojects. Latin America and the Far East fall somewhere in between the two extremes.

In 1975, there were numerous articles recounting details of the clogged ports, labor shortages, and enormous logistical problems resulting from the numerous projects simultaneously underway in the Middle East. Many of the enormous cost escalations were directly caused by severe shortages of capital goods, infrastructural facilities and manpower. Competition among developing countries to access these material inputs for growth was intense in the 1970s. The more projects there were underway at the same time, the more difficult it seemed to be to maintain cost and time commitments.

BEYOND THE CAPABILITIES OF A SINGLE ORGANIZATION

The sheer magnitude of these Third World projects makes them a strain as well as a challenge; the skills and talents that must be engaged call for major feats of coordination and planning. The enormous differences in business styles and in national and regional objectives and goals makes project teams extremely difficult to pull together and organize. The wide divergence of skills and capabilities that individual participants can bring to bear on a project creates a broad range of alternative partnership approaches requiring highly sophisticated appraisal.

Developing countries offer on the one hand rich and, as yet, untapped resources while, on the other hand they are dependent for further economic growth on vast infrastructure development, and frequently lack managerial and technological capabilities. The huge gap between their potential and what developing countries are independently capable of undertaking offers a call and a challenge to businessmen of many industries and nationalities possessing technological knowledge and managerial experience. The organizations which have responded to this challenge have had unique expertise which varied in importance to the host, depending upon the requirements of the particular project.

Transnational Contributions the Norm

Today's projects in the developing world are usually collaborative efforts between organizations in the host country (whether local company, parastatal or state enterprise, or government ministry) and one or more guest multinationals. The mutual interdependence is verified by the structure of the population of participating companies: host versus guest companies are equally represented, although the population by company industry is quite varied.

Depending on their nature and scope, the projects in developing countries may attract:

1. Resource companies — hydrocarbon processing, metal, pulp and paper. Among the resource companies active on the survey projects, there is a fairly balanced mix between host and guest participants. The host has the resource supply; either host or guest (or both) may have the demand; and the guest typically has the technology to support the project.

2. <u>Goods and services companies</u> — engineering and construction, equipment manufacturers, trading companies. Here the mix is skewed toward the guest because the host usually lacks the necessary technology to compete at the high technology end, although host companies are making inroads at the low technology end.

3. <u>Public administration and infrastructure companies</u> — communications, utilities, transport. In the macroproject sample, host companies outnumber guests either because the country must maintain national sovereignty through majority equity of these projects and/or because it is sponsoring the development.

Of all the guest companies, nearly 80 percent come from just six OECD nations — Japan, the United States, West Germany, the United Kingdom, Italy, and France. Companies from these nations represent well over half the total number of companies providing capital goods and engineering, construction, and other services to macroprojects (Figure 1.4).

These companies, whether hosts or guests, participate in the development of these projects either on an equity or contractual basis. The lead, and therefore major, responsibilities on these macroprojects fall to the owners of the operating facility and to those who assume managerial control during the project preparation and construction period. It is the owners who, at the outset, define the project concept to meet a specific perceived market demand. Ownership requires involvement early on in project formulation, identification, and feasibility — and in defining the economics of the project, relative to existing and future markets.

Subsequently, these players are faced with the task of sourcing the appropriate technology and constructing the planned facility. Typically, owners also maintain managerial or supervisory authority over the project during construction. Owners presently have several other alternatives open to them, depending upon the extent of their reliance on support from international engineers, constructors, and/or equipment manufacturers. Owners can: (1) undertake the project themselves — maintaining responsibility for management of operational as well as developmental aspects of the project (or sharing it with joint venture partners); (2) maintain only authority to review and approve by contracting out the project preparation

Figure 1.4

A. Mix of Participating Companies - 3052 in Total

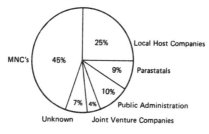

B. Major Company Industries:

Rank	Company Type		OECD - Six As % Total
1.	Equipment Manufacturer:	Electrical	73%
2.	Equipment Manufacturer:	Non-Electrical	68
3.	Trading		58
4.	Other Manufacture		58
5.	Engineering/Construction		57
6.	Communications		55
7.	Transport		34
8.	Conglomerate		33
9.	Steel		30
10.	Fuel: Oil/Gas		28
11.	Aluminum		27
12.	Petrochemical/Chemical		27
13.	Other Metals		26
14.	Pulp & Paper		21
15.	Utilities		12
16.	Copper		10
17	Public Administration		4

C. Companies From Six Major OECD Countries As Percent of Total Companies Active

MNC's	No. of Companies	Local Host	No. of Companies	Parastatals	No. of Companies
Engineering/ Construction	509	Metal	199	Fuel: Oil/Gas	54
		Petrochem/Chemical	126	Utilities	35
Equipment Mfg.	109	Engineering/		Petrochem/Chemical	31
Metal	147	Construction	106		
Finance/Banking	98	Fuel: Oil/Gas	78		
Petrochem/Chemical	93				
Fuel: Oil/Gas	88				

work to international consulting or design engineers and/or the construction work to contractors; or (3) delegate project management authority by contracting out the complete job (by unit, entire system, or plant), to either a turnkey contractor, a turnkey

Table 1.2

Bargaining Power of Prospective Participants

Leverage Equation	Capital Sourcing	Technology Transfer	Market Access
Low host leverage High guest leverage	- Insufficient local capital - Unpredictability of cost estimates - Availability of supplies/other credits	- Introduction of a new industry - Exclusivity technology	- No local market demand for output - No access to inter-national markets
Low guest leverage High host leverage	- Sufficient local capital - Predictability of cost estimates	- Developed local industry/expertise - Local production of capital goods	- Developed local market demand - International market experience/channels - Scarcity of resource

contractors' consortium, or a project manager (design-constructor).

In the first instance, technology is sourced either locally or via the joint venture partners(s). In the second, multiple contracts are written to fulfill the various technological requirements, whether design, engineering, equipment supply or construction. In the third case, managerial and supervisory control is delegated to the turnkey contractors who supply a complete package of services — from design, procurement, training and construction to start-up.

Bargaining Leverage Varies

Before a determination can be made on the ultimate scope of a potential project and the package of outside skills and resources that will need to be pulled together to undertake it, an assessment of the availability of local resources must be made.

For projects with high financial risk and up-front capital requirements, such as mining, capital sourcing might be the most important variable. For chemicals, the question of market access might be the overriding factor. For projects with high technological requirements, such as electric power or telecommunications, technology transfer might be the crucial factor in deciding the nature of the project and whether to proceed.

In an infrastructure project, the issue of international market access would not arise, as there is no output to be sold on world markets, but there might well be capital sourcing and technological sourcing difficulties. It may be easy, for example, to understand how Saudi Arabia can afford a $20 billion industrial city (i.e. petrodollars), but it is more difficult to imagine where adequate managerial and technological capabilities and resources might be found. In contrast, international market access is critical to undertaking the production of large volumes of an indigenous resource for which there is little local demand, such as Asahan's large-scale aluminum project in Indonesia.

As host and guest companies are drawn into the negotiation process, they begin to undertake specific commitments to the project. The distribution of risk and responsibility among them is determined by the bargaining power of each, which depends, in turn, on how essential its contributions to the project will be. As each of the project requirements is considered, the bargaining powers of the prospective participants begin to emerge.

Table 1.3

Top Twenty Macroproject Participants

Rank	Participant Organization	Contractual Commitments	Typical Mode of Involvement
1	World Bank	93	Financing
2	Mitsubishi,* Japan	88	Equity Joint Venture; Contractor's Consortium
3	Mitsui,* Japan	66	Contractors' Consortium; Equity Joint Venture
4	Saudi Arabian Gov't.	53	Sole Owner
5	Pullman-Kellogg, U.S.	48	Project Manager; Contractor; Consultant/Tech. Asst.
6	Bechtel,* U.S.	39	Contractor; Project Manager; Consultant/Tech. Asst.
7	C. Itoh, Japan	39	Contractors' Consortium; Equity Joint Venture
8	Royal Dutch Shell,* Neth./UK	36	Equity Joint Venture; Project Manager
9	Snam Progetti, Italy	35	Contractors' Consortium; Project Manager; Contractor
10	Sonatrach, Algeria	33	Sole Owner
11	Fluor,* U.S.	32	Project Manager; Contractor; Consultant/Tech. Asst.
12	Iranian Government	30	Sole Owner
13	Egyptian Government	28	Sole Owner
14	Uhde, F., W. Germany	26	Turnkey Contractor
15	Foster Wheeler, U.S.	23	Contractor
16	CVRD, Brazil	23	Equity Joint Venture; Sole Owner
17	Pemex, Mexico	22	Sole Owner
18	National Iran Oil Co.	22	Sole Owner
19	Nippon Steel, Japan	22	Long-Term Purchase; Consultant/Tech. Asst.
20	Toyo Engineering, Japan	22	Contractor

* - Total organization.

Hosts and guests each approach the bargaining table with certain negotiating strengths and weaknesses that result not from who they are, but what they potentially can contribute. The variables which define this power profile are described in Table 1.2.

In general, the host participant approaches the bargaining table with certain strengths: It can set ownership limits and, if it is a government, it can often dictate the tax treatment of project participants, and the percentage of labor and capital goods that must be sourced locally — in other words, control the environment in which the project is positioned. Weaknesses may be the host's inability to meet the high development costs of the project, lack of sufficient local markets, dependence on foreign capital and technology, or a combination of these factors.

Guest multinationals who are interested in participation as owners have the option of hedging their exposure via participation in multiple projects. They may also have a certain ascendancy because of their capacity to absorb project output by marketing it in their home countries or on the world market. Their need for the raw material supply may weaken their bargaining position, however. And depending on the project outcome and host-country conditions, they may risk potential impairment of earning power or seizure of assets.

Guest multinationals who are interested in participating on a contractual basis have the option of assembling a complete fixed-fee package of engineering/construction services, providing management expertise, or simply designing or constructing the project under a separate contract. The multinational's decision is based upon the capabilities and needs of the host sponsors.

In summary, for each project, participating companies contribute partially or wholly to any or all of the three central requirements: (1) capital; (2) technology; and (3) market access. They satisfy these requirements through equity and/or contractual commitments. A look at the typical mode of involvement of the top 20 macroproject participants (based on number of contractual commitments) shows the diversity of support being provided to macroprojects (Table 1.3). The top twenty companies include seven host enterprises (35%) (Saudi Arabian, Iranian and Egyptian Government Ministeries, Sonatrach, CVRD, Pemex and National Iranian Oil Co.), six of whom participate principally as sole owners; five Japanese corporations (25%) (Mitsubishi, Mitsui, C. Itoh, Nippon

Steel and Toyo Engineering), three of whom participate typically as joint venturers or in a consortium of contractors; four U.S. firms (Pullman Kellogg, Bechtel, Fluor and Foster Wheeler), all of whom are noted for their project management capability, although they are also frequently awarded independent contracts; three European, (including Shell, with worldwide equity commitments; Snamprogetti, with consortia and project management involvement; and Uhde with numerous turnkey contracts); and one international lending agency, the World Bank, involved in project financing. This list is based on absolute number of contracts, and makes no attempt to weight them by comparative complexity. The types of commitments are so diverse, a reliable weighting would be hard to develop. The flexibility of these lead participants in accepting whole or partial contracts is providing enormous support to Third World development.

DIFFICULT TO CONTROL

Just a look at the many facets of these macroprojects that need to be coordinated attests to their complexity: the enormous feasibility, design, and engineering requirements; the intricate and protracted negotiations and legal arrangements necessary to source adequate technology, materials, and skills; the complications of project financing; the elaborate project management organization and staffing; the enormous local labor training effort; and finally, the vast infrastructure that almost invariably must be built to support a macroproject. These undertakings are engaging the very best of host and multinational talent and skills.

Nevertheless, multinationals are continually finding that projects that ran smoothly in an industrialized environment are frought with difficulties and risks in the Third World. Evidence of these difficulties can be found in the rampant cost escalations, completion delays, and postponements or suspensions. More surprising than the fact that problems occur is the magnitude of these problems. Macroprojects run into more than their share of trouble, however, some difficulties are external to the project, and therefore beyond management's capability to control; while others are internal to the project, and therefore within management's sphere of control.

Cost/Time Overruns Common

Cost escalations and completion delays are quite common on Third World macroprojects. Looking at all projects with problems, the average cost escalation falls between 100 and 149 percent, and the typical completion delay runs from between 1 to 2 years. (Longer delays are not uncommon, however.) (Table 1.4)

Table 1.4

Distribution of Troubled Projects By Magnitude of Trouble

Cost Escalations		Completion Delays	
Percent Escalation	Percent of Projects	Number Of Years	Percent of Projects
200+%	17%	5 +	8%
150-199	11	3-4	26
100-149	67	1-2	65
25- 99	5	1	2

Overall, escalations and delays vary with the total capital cost of a project: This research indicates that the likelihood of experiencing cost escalations, completion delays, and postponements or suspensions increases with the size of the project — the more complex the project, the more troublesome (Figure 1.5). Cost

Figure 1.5

Trouble Rate by Project Size

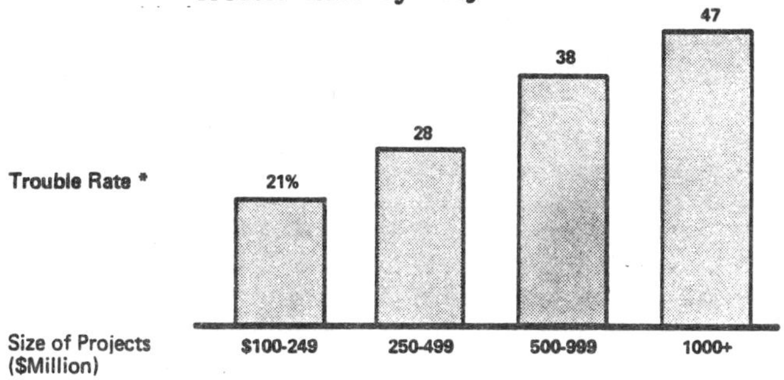

Size of Projects ($Million)	$100-249	250-499	500-999	1000+
Trouble Rate *	21%	28	38	47

Percentage of total

Cost Escalation	10%	18	28	34
Postponed/Suspended	7	10	13	20
Completion Delay	11	14	16	16
Revivals	2	3	5	8
Average cost escalation	30%	70	106	109

*Percentage of total projects in size range with cost escalations, completion delays, postponements/suspensions.

escalations averaged 30 percent on the smaller macroprojects, but 109 percent on the larger projects. These were usually accompanied by, or the result of, postponements, suspensions, or completion delays. On the other hand, the likelihood of revival after postponement or suspension is also greatest for the largest projects.

Often, cost escalations and completion delays are interrelated. According to Hydrocarbon Processing, a one-month delay will mean an increase of 4 to 6 percent in the total capital cost of the project (i.e., 48 to 72 percent per year) carried out in the United States. The study indicated that an overrun is not a function of the time planned for construction nor the size or nature of the facility, but rather of the cost of money and the rate of return. For a $100 million project the cost overrun would be $4 million to $6 million per month delay, or $200,000 per day. In the macroproject survey, escalations and delays have been found to be interrelated, with percent escalation tending to increase with number of years delayed (Table 1.5).

Table 1.5

Distribution of Delayed Projects by Percent Escalation

Percent Escalation	Completion Delays			
	1 Year	2 Years	3 Years	4 Years
Below 100%	6%	3%	3%	5%
100 - 150	72	70	67	48
150 - 200	9	11	15	14
200 - up	13	16	15	33

In light of these findings, the planning stage is clearly a major concern. Prospective sponsors can avoid some of these problems by developing a sound project concept with reasonable project economics. The risks that threaten these economics are usually associated with: (1) competitive threats or constraints encountered in integrating the project within the local or global industry, or (2) the complexity of the project itself.

Factors Beyond Management's Control

More than anything, high risk is equivalent to high level of vulnerability to external factors that are beyond the control of project participants and can delay or have the potential of delaying a project at some point during its lifecycle. Fluctuations in market conditions, inflation, and exchange rates rank high among the external causes of cost escalations, completion delays, and postponements or suspensions. Because of the serious impact of these external factors, environmental evaluation is critical.

Changing market conditions were the single most important factor in the repeated postponements and revivals of a multibillion dollar petrochemical plant in Saudi Arabia, for example. Originally slated to produce 500,000 tons of ethylene per year, the plant was eventually scaled down because of reduced demand for the output, and the start-up date was strategically repositioned to match the expected rise in market demand. (Table 1.6)

Table 1.6

Status History of a Saudi Arabian Petrochemical Project

Announcement Date	Project Status	Cost Estimate ($ Billions)	Estimated Date of Completion
1970	Planned	$1	1980
1973	Postponed		
1974	Revived	3	?
1975	Negotiated	3	?
1976	Postponed		
1977	Revived	2*	1985
1977	Agreed	2	1985

* — Scaled down.

Perhaps the most afflicted project to date is the Saudi Arabian Gas Gathering System, a pipeline designed to deliver 5.5 billion cubic feet of gas per day. Between 1974 when the project was announced and 1977 when the contracts were let, Saudi Arabia experienced an inflation rate of nearly 98 percent — or roughly 33 percent per year. During that time estimates of project costs increased 433 percent, and the completion date was pushed farther into the future (Table 1.7).

Table 1.7

Cost History of a Saudi Arabian Gas Gathering Project: Planning Stage Only

Announcement Date	Cost Estimate ($ Billions)	Estimated Date Of Completion
July 1974	$ 3.0	1979
January 1976	4.0	1979
January 1976	4.5	1980
August 1976	10.0	1981
September 1976	15.0	1984
February 1977	16.0	1985

These changes, however, were only changes "on paper" because they occurred during the planning stage. It is far better to develop a more exact definition of the project than to wait until the work is under way. Once the contracts and commitments have been signed, the discovery that the project will require four times more capital than previously estimated will have disastrous consequences for the viability of the project. The Saudi persistence in developing accurate scope, cost, and market entry dates is an example of sound project preparation.

Some typical risks that are beyond the scope of management's control, and their attendant problems and impact, are listed below. The graver these risks and the higher their likelihood, the more leverage the guest sponsor may have in project negotiation.

1. Risks which are related to project complexity include:
   • Unpredictable development costs (i.e., mining projects when the mineral is in an inaccessible location; or of the wrong gravity, and therefore require additional facilities for processing)
   • Unpredictable infrastructure costs (i.e., when a resource project is located in a remote area or green site)

2. Other risks are related to the domestic and/or international competitiveness of the project, such as:

- Inaccessible market for the output (i.e., most resource industries are vertically integrated, with little open trading)
- Failure to achieve economies of scale (i.e., a large plant capacity may be required to achieve a competitive price, but a guarantee of a high rate of utilization is essential to sound economics)
- Need for exclusive technology (i.e., the more exclusive the technology required for completion of the project the higher the percent equity required to guarantee the guest an adequate rate of return)
- Uncertainty of return on capital invested (i.e., on high-risk projects providers of capital may demand foreign equity or control as a precautionary measure).

Since complex external conditions have implications for the kinds of financing, equity, and marketing arrangements required to support the project, as well as its plant capacity, the accurate assessment of these factors during the planning stage is critical to the success of a project.

Factors Within Management's Control

During the development lifecycle of a project, there are many factors that contribute directly to cost escalations, completion delays, and postponements or suspensions. Among them are: the inability to estimate logistical risks; insufficient up-front labor, procurement, and time/budget planning; difficulties in implementing designs given local climatic and other conditions; ignorance of local cultural constraints and value conflicts; as well as inappropriate management and control systems and procedures during construction — which must be carefully correlated with a number of decisions and activities that must be carried out concurrently. Any of these internal risks or threats have implications for the kind of design, construction, and project management arrangements to be found.

While pitfalls indeed lurk at every stage in the project lifecycle, the further along the project, the more likely it is to have encountered difficulty. Figure 1.6 shows the distribution of

Figure 1.6

Breakdown of Troubled Projects by Stage of Development

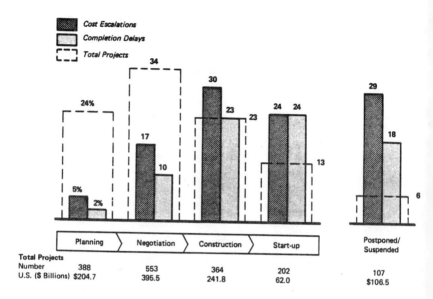

macroprojects, as well as the distribution of cost escalations and completion delays to date by current status. In fact, the construction phase seems to be the most difficult: it is at that time that the greatest concentration of capital and resources are expended, making any errors in sequencing highly costly.

A review of some of the difficulties which are likely to be encountered by guest multinationals is helpful in understanding the causes of project delays and the measures which can be taken to prevent them. Overall, the greatest single error made by foreign contractors lies in a failure to take local conditions into account. Because these macroprojects are highly visible, national events, they can be disruptive to the local communities. In many cases, pressures are intensified by the fact that there are numerous macroprojects going on in a single country or location — straining the infrastructure, taxing the local labor supply, as well as local manufacturing capabilities. In cases where macroprojects are being built on green-sites in remote locations, a combination of logistical and sociological difficulties can put considerable pressure on the project manager to supply motivation and strong and consistent direction. The pitfalls a foreign contractor might face begin with the design of the facility and end only when the facility has been completely — and successfully — started up (Table 1.8). Some of the unexpected problems which occurred during the 1970s are described below.

1. Design and engineering can be problematic when collaboration is required on an international basis:

- The indigenous climate may be overlooked. For example, design engineers of a metal processing plant in South East Asia failed to make allowances for the dry wind storms occurring in the area. The storms caused dust which interfered with the turbine generator. Ammonia seepage eroded the equipment. Correction of this design error cost the owners an additional $30 to $40 million. The plant operated at less than 50 percent capacity utilization for more than three years after start-up until the necessary corrections could be made.

- Local costs of materials may differ from international costs. On a pulp and paper project in South America, the multinational participants specified carbon steel which was equivalent in price to stainless steel in their home country. In the host country carbon steel was three times more expensive, greatly (and unnecessarily) increasing construction costs. All materials had to be respecified, causing delays.

2. Logistical and procurement problems may be unusually difficult, due to the fact that macroprojects are frequently located in remote and often inaccessible areas. This creates enormous problems in coordinating materials flow, communications, etc.

- Communication networks may be non-existent. In one instance, not only was the head office of an Asian metal processing plant located two days' travel time away from the smelter and power sites, there also were no telephones, making it impossible to track day-to-day needs and make timely deliveries. Until a communications network could be installed, the sequencing of the project was poor, causing the project to fall behind schedule.

Table 1.8

Typical Project Management Pitfalls

Major Project Management Risks	Typical Problems	Impact	
		Schedule	Budget
Inappropriate design/engineering	• Unique climate conditions	X	X
	• Unexpected costs in meeting local specs		
Inadequate procurement	• Logistical problems	X	
	• Insufficient servicing of equipment	X	
	• Inadequate quality standards—whether int'l or local	X	
Inadequate labor force to achieve schedule/budget commitments	• Lack of adeaute labor supply or of skilled labor	X	X
	• Differences in wages from one region to another	X	
	• Effect of local cultural habits on productivity	X	
Difficulty in assessing option least detrimental to budget/schedule	• Sequencing problems	X	
	• Trade-off cost of potential delays against cost of		
	– Additional precautions	±	±
	– Additional investment	±	±
Weak interface with local community	• Site clearance problems	X	X
	• Social isolation, crime		

- Overpurchase of materials and equipment is not an uncommon approach to overcompensating for difficult logistics. When a metal processing project was completed and millions of dollars of unused material and equipment were left behind, the owners were clearly irate — but they were also at a loss as to what to do with the excess. The owners were forced to market these items to other projects underway in the country.
- Quality standards of locally manufactured equipment may not comply with those required of international exporters. Parts to be used in a project in South America and manufactured locally were faulty, requiring replacement; because the defects were not discovered until startup, the project was delayed.

3. Labor coordination can be difficult. The mix of expatriates and indigenous workers of urban and regional origins requires some skill to coordinate.

- Conflicts or arguments among expatriates and locals, or between the owners and the project manager, can cause high turnover, reassignments, and will invariably result in costly delays.
- Local labor cost differentials from urban to rural areas can make budgeting difficult. While wages in rural areas may be higher than in urban areas because of scarcity of labor, budgets generally are based on urban wages.
- Local customs can affect performance. Religious fasts, superstitions, lack of experience in working with machinery or driving a motor vehicle, for example, can slow productivity.

4. Overall sequencing is sometimes overlooked. Equipment, for example, might be ordered too early or too late, disturbing the overall project schedule — but definitely increasing costs.

- Equipment order and delivery preceded the agreement by joint venture partners to go ahead with an Asian gas processing project. Five tankers worth $1.8 billion were delivered two years before they were needed. They had to begin paying for them — including interest on loans — as they sat in the harbor, waiting for the project to reach completion.

When capital goods and engineering/construction services are sourced from around the world, expertise in integrating the goods and services with local approaches and systems can make the difference between completion on target or costly overruns.

SOCIALLY AND CULTURALLY INCONGRUOUS

The enormous efforts at transnational and transcorporate collaboration required to implement these macroprojects are far more complex than the nature of the agreement between the owners, project managers and government officials. An important factor in the loss of control of these projects involves the large number of stakeholders participating in and surrounding the project, and the enormous gulf in social and cultural values and modes of operation among each group. A striking aspect of these macroprojects is the human side — the linkages between managers from different cultures, their need to work on highly sophisticated technology with highly inexperienced labor; their need to clear local communities off the sites to erect highly complex facilities; their need to manage conflicts among foreigners in a remote location.

The nature of these differences in values, perspectives, and work approaches will be described in this section. These variables deserve serious attention by project planners, as they have implications for the way in which the project's management and control functions can best be organized. The cultural gaps can be so profound that one can only marvel at the magnitude of what has been achieved to date.

Partners: The Moslem and the Oriental

Japanese and Indonesians formed a joint venture to build a world-scale aluminum smelter and hydroelectric plant in Sumatra. It appeared to be a rewarding business arrangement. The Japanese were to provide highly exclusive technology and financing (some at low interest rates). They also agreed to purchase 100% of the output on a long-term basis. The Indonesians were to provide the smelter and hydroelectric plant sites, the most powerful waterfall in the world, and local labor. The equity split was 90% Japanese, 10% Indonesian.

Serious difficulties arose, however, when implementation of the project began. The essential requirements of a real team effort seemed to be missing.

In day-to-day matters, there was no common ground between the Japanese and Indonesians; even their food was different. The Japanese liked fresh, light foods with delicate seasoning; the Indonesians liked heavily spiced foods — appropriate in their hot climate, but a shock to the unaccustomed palate. Their languages were different: the Japanese spoke their native tongue and some English; the Indonesians spoke Bahasa and some English. A translator stood between them. Their concepts of time were different: the Japanese were punctual; the Indonesians believed in "rubber time."

In addition, their concepts of authority were not alike: the Japanese have a moral loyalty to their masters, who, in turn, always remain faithful to the welfare of the whole. The Indonesians find it difficult to unquestioningly follow the dictates of a manager, for only 20 or 30 years ago their masters were colonizers. In addition, their approaches to decision-making are different. While both seek consensus, the Japanese reach it in such a way that no one man appears to be responsible for managing a project. The Indonesians will give the appearance of having arrived at a consensus because of their reluctance to challenge an authority figure.

The character of their commitments also differs. The Japanese dedicate their lives to their companies, and are surprised that the Indonesians will change jobs for higher pay. The Indonesians are very religious, i.e., the Moslems on this project fasted during one month, and were near the fainting point by the end of the day. From their perspective, the Japanese seemed to have no religion at all.

The only way that they would be able to work effectively together is through the culture, spirit, and organizational structure of the joint venture company. Project planners need to give careful thought to how to organize the decision-making process to avoid conflicts or problems based purely on personal differences. It was impressive to see the amount of concern on both sides regarding their differences — and their mutual hope of making a success of the project.

Co-Workers: The Caveman and the Oilman

One of the world's major oil companies and one of the major engineering/construction firms were required to use only local

Indonesian labor to construct and operate one of the most sophisticated plants with state-of-the-art technology.

The discrepancy between the people they thought they needed and the available manpower seemed enormous. The plant had to be built within a short time-frame, yet even in the industrialized countries training for the required technical jobs requires training periods as long as four years.

Labor is a key factor in completing these macroprojects in developing countries on time at estimated cost. Labor costs accumulate directly in man-days and indirectly in capital equipment costs. Any variation due to delays or strikes has a bottom-line impact. Therefore, having a sufficient number of laborers available and keeping them on the job is critical for success.

In the Third World, the labor requirements are higher, because the most modern equipment cannot be used (for lack of skilled labor), and productivity is lower (because of the debilitating climate). There is little variation in the speeds of various skilled workers, but unskilled workers are considerably slower; concrete work, for example, takes an Indonesian worker four hours as compared with an hour for a worker in the United States.

There are many surprises, nevertheless. Badak people — very primitive, totally uneducated, unable to read, from the jungle, the rain forest, unchanged since the beginning of time — were taken straight out of the jungle and given a major oil company's aptitude tests to determine their ability to learn various job skills. The scores recorded by the Badaks were the highest ever recorded, indicating that the Badaks were highly trainable. Most foreigners were amazed at their ability to pick up a sophisticated technology rapidly.

Not all workers in the Third World are as highly trainable. It is true that people in developing countries are more manually dexterous. However, they also may often lack discipline. For example, those who have spent their lives as fishermen may be attracted to construction by the higher income, but may be resistant to the change in life-style.

It is up to the owners and project management contractors to set up adequate training programs for indigenous workers to bring their various skill levels up to some measure of consistency. Often, these formal programs provide the only alternative for meeting the local labor quota requirements.

Neighbors: The Agrarian and the Industrialist

Macroprojects are intended to contribute to the industrialization of developing countries. Change is to be expected. The
value systems within local communities require considerable respect
and careful management. The significance of this reality becomes
clear at the moment of site preparation.

In developing a macroproject, the sponsors — whether host or
multinational companies — need to be aware of how best to manage
site preparation, how to get indigenous people involved in the
project, and how to manage the transition from construction to
operation.

Their purposes are different: the locals regard the land as a
heritage — that which holds their history, their roots, their
identities; the industrializers, on the other hand, see the land as a
site to be cleared — the basis for creating the future, the low-cost
item upon which a great wealth-generating facility will be constructed.

The landholders must be considered. A Papua, New Guinea
copper project was planning to mine minerals in a local tribe's
territory. An Indonesian aluminum smelter required that a Sumatran
tribe be displaced. Without concessions on the parts of landholders,
sites cannot be cleared, and projects cannot go ahead.

The management of site clearance varies in difficulty. The
Badak area was a virgin jungle already acquired by the host
enterprise. Nevertheless, some natives returned after the site had
been cleared and planted new crops. The government allowed them
to harvest the crops before taking the land.

In contrast, the tribe in Sumatra attributed religious significance to the roots of the trees, which — they believed — connected
them to their ancestry. In their minds, site clearance was a
disturbance of a gravesite.

Local residents may ask inflated prices for the land at the
time of clearance, even though the people may be squatters
themselves. The governments, nevertheless, pay them for the
property and provide resettlement land.

The project leaders need to exercise great care in creating an
understanding and acceptance of the project as early on as possible.
Once the site is cleared, their further cooperation will be needed.
The project organization therefore requires a capability to manage
cultural change on an ongoing basis.

Visitors: The Marginal Man and the Member

The construction of a macroproject requires that thousands of expatriates be transplanted to the site to put the facility in place. Regardless of whether the project is on a "green site" or near an existing community, new housing may be required to accommodate the large volume of people, and completely new work camps or communities may have to be built.

The expatriates — or "expats," as they frequently call themselves — are out of their element, living on the fringes of a strange environment. The conditions are tough; the climate is often hot; tropical diseases are common. Medical problems are intensified, due to a shortage of doctors and hospitals. A water supply must be developed and food has to be provided, in the right quantity and type. In Badak, reefers carried meat and vegetables from Bali, as very little food could be grown locally, due to the poor soil. People were carried in by helicopters and boats until the airstrip was completed. As is common in most "marginal" situations, social unrest is widespread, leading to alcoholism, divorce, boredom, supermarket complaints, fist-fights, and sometimes even murder.

Thus, the project manager must somehow create a sense of community among these expats to diminish the sense of social isolation. The project manager must, in fact, install an entire community before even beginning the construction of the project.

The previous discussion demonstrates the need to analyze all the implications of such an enormous endeavor before a macroproject is undertaken. Proposing projects of "macro" dimensions requires that project participants be willing to struggle at the frontiers of management and technology. To develop the very largest projects known to date, breakthroughs or adaptations are essential. Current management systems do not provide adequate measures of flexibility and complexity to deal with all the variables that affect the success or failure of macroprojects in the Third World. The network of collaborative efforts of public and private enterprises of all types from all countries makes timely negotiations and decision-making essential. Beyond the players directly involved, projects of this scale can seriously and permanently change "the way things are done" in an industry, country, region, etc. — resulting in serious social and economic discontinuities. The remaining chapters discuss some important aspects of transnational collaboration — the success of which is crucial to mastering the complexity of these projects.

2
Host as Macroproject Customer

The host countries and the entities/agencies who make the decisions to invest at a macroproject level have a significant and direct influence on demand for macroprojects as a function of their responsibility for national development plans and industrial development sectoral strategies.

The nature of the demand for macroprojects by host countries is constantly changing, as host entities themselves are being continuously trained and enriched by their macroproject activities and partnerships. Host entities evaluated and made the purchase of extensive engineering and construction services and capital goods with the support, financing and investment of carefully selected multinational equity partners over the last decade: With over 1600 projects worth more than $1 trillion having been planned or constructed, the Third World can no longer be regarded as naive purchasers of macroproject technology.

Host countries, as a group, seem to have maintained the image or reputation of being politically turbulent, cavalier about contractual agreements, and given to abrupt nationalization of industries. They are often regarded as high risk, or highly unreliable business partners. A focused examination of the macroproject arena provides quite a different impression of their business competencies.

Third World activities are typically analyzed by country or by industry segment. When macroprojects are treated as a distinct market segment, with industrial and infrastructural projects treated as subsegments of that market, interesting host buying patterns begin to emerge, namely, 1) higher income host countries are purchasing the bulk of macroprojects; 2) their portfolios with respect to the industrial/infrastructural elements are diverse; and 3) host buyers as a group are becoming increasingly more sophisticated.

HIGHER INCOME COUNTRIES PURCHASE MORE

Income level is commonly regarded as an important indicator of level of development. Economic or industrial development can be viewed as a process of steadily increasing per capita income, much like the evolution of a new industry or market. A country goes through several development stages: pretransition; take-off; transition, or high growth; and finally the country arrives at a point of industrialization or maturity. Each country stands somewhere on a continuum that leads, at the highest level, to a per capita income or gross national product (GNP) equivalent to that of OECD countries.

The process of development or industrialization is much like rubbing two pieces of wood together to build a fire: it is commonly believed that with enough intense stimulation, any developing economy will suddenly ignite, and that the resulting momentum will ensure steady and consistent economic growth.

Over the last decade, some countries have been able to stimulate such development in an impressive way, while other countries have been left far behind. One need only compare the 1970 and 1979 World Bank annual reports (i.e., pre- and post-oil crisis) to notice the enormous progress — and lack of progress — that took place over that period. Where once countries were divided by region, there are now entirely new categorizations for Third World countries: "Newly industrialized countries," "OPEC"; "resource-rich developing", "poor-I", "Poor-II", "Poor-III".

The belief that the poor are being left further behind appears to be supported by the macroproject survey findings. The macroproject sample confirms that macroprojects are tools for the higher income developing countries to advance their growth objectives. The distribution of macroprojects by per capita income levels of host countries demonstrates that the higher income countries are making greater commitments to macroproject development (Figure 2.1). In this connection, the projects with the largest average investment costs are underway in the higher-income developing countries (over $2000 per capita) such as Saudi Arabia, and of course Australia and New Zealand, accounting for 17 percent of all countries. About half of all macroproject activity is taking place in medium-income developing countries ($500 to $1,999 per capita) such as Brazil, Iran, and Iraq. Lower-income countries ($200 - $499 per capita) have a number of projects which represent a small average investment size per project. Relatively few macroprojects are taking place in the lowest-income countries (less than $200 per capita) such as Bangladesh and Afghanistan.

Figure 2.1

**Distribution of Macroprojects
By Host Country Per Capita Income**

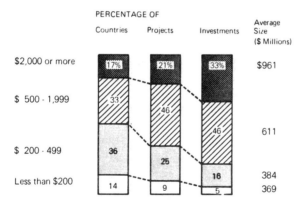

DIVERSE PORTFOLIOS

Much progress can be made in advancing the national development goals of a country by means of macroproject-scale initiatives. One project can install a nationwide highway, telecommunications system or launch an entirely new industrial sector. Macroprojects have been used as a tool for the more fervently aggressive Third World governments seeking extremely rapid industrialization. These governments are willing to exploit their strongest resources or assets, whether minerals to be extracted, or manpower for labor-intensive industry, to generate sufficient capital to roll-over into other economic sectors viewed as vital to full industrialization.

In fact, there do seem to be specific steps and sequencing of projects that are important to growth. To industrialize: 1) The mix of national production needs to be structurally shifted from predominantly agricultural to predominantly industrial; 2) Infrastructural supports, such as electricity, transportation, and communications networks, must be put in place at certain per capita income levels if the right impetus to growth is to be achieved; and 3) Large concentrations of the population must be shifted from rural to urban locations. This requires that water and sewage systems, housing, hospitals, schools, etc. be put in place at the right time to support and encourage this flow of human resources.

Host governments decide on the redistribution of capital and rechanneling of investment by means of their three to five year development plans. These plans map out the sectoral strategies for individual industry or infrastructure sectors and defines how the sectors relate to each other. This is a very important and difficult responsibility of the host governments. Nevertheless, this task must be done, as governments who fail to effectively rechannel investment may in fact permanently hamper development.

Developing countries have different criteria for assessing the appropriateness of a macroproject. Host sponsors often have objectives which are broader than the economic attractiveness of the projects. They seek to justify the project in terms of its industrial sector impact as well as its fit in the overall national development program. Their concept of risk has different meanings depending on the purpose of the project in terms of its interface with the local and global industry, and the extent to which it contributes to the country's overall development.

The industrial sector strategy addresses issues of economies of scale and evaluates opportunities to maximize value-added from indigenous resources by means of forward and backward linkages, whenever possible. Host sponsors' concepts of adequate economies of scale are influenced by the size of the home market, the resulting export objectives, and practices in the global industry regarding ownership and marketing of output. The larger countries can be more independent in sponsoring a project, since the output of a facility can be absorbed by the domestic market. Smaller countries may need to enter into joint ventures to market the output and thus achieve scale economies. Some facilities, such as LNG and ethylene facilities, invariably involve investments greater than $100 million; others, such as textiles, cement, and many downstream petrochemicals, are typically smaller than $100 million in size. Similarly, larger countries are more likely to integrate forward or backward because of the potential for creating demand within their large home market. The metal and hydrocarbon processing industries are the principle candidates for such integration.

The national development plan allows for certain development priorities to be identified and implemented. Such priorities might include evaluating a project's contribution to government revenues, foreign exchange, and/or upgrading of local labor through skills transfer before giving the go ahead. Whether and how a project contributes to national development can be a more decisive factor than the bottom line of a traditional cost/benefit analysis. Host governments have been known to strategically position a project so that it provides the maximum development benefits to the country by locating it in a depressed area to develop a region and stimulate growth regardless of the economic consequences. An example is the Pronorte Polypropylene project that was to be situated in Camacari, in the northeastern petrochemical zone of Bahia. The government obliged Pronorte to relocate the project to the Sao Paulo petrochemical zone in order to utilize propane from the expanded naptha cracking from a refinery located there, even though it meant an increase in investment from $24 million to $150 million.

Any group of developing countries will prove to have distinctive purchasing approaches, when compared to one another, as their history, size, location, position along the industrialization or development continuum will affect what projects they are interested in, how they are willing and able to support and participate in them, and what kinds of services they will look to multinationals to provide.

Volume of Activity

Macroprojects are not typically developed in a sequence, one at a time. Six percent of the developing nations have 50 or more macroprojects proposed or underway, representing close to half of the total investment (Figure 2.2). The investment size of their projects averages about $850 million. An additional 13 percent of the host countries have a third of all the macroprojects within their

38

Figure 2.2

Distribution of Macroprojects
By Host Country Portfolio Size

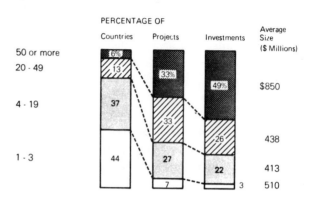

borders, but these projects are half the size of the segment with
larger portfolios, that is about $438 million. Another 37 percent of
the host countries have 4 to 19 macroprojects within their borders,
with an average size similar to the previous group. Other countries
have few macroprojects: 44 percent of the developing nations with
macroprojects have portfolios which include only one to three
macroprojects.

Type of Activity

Macroprojects do not develop only one resource in a country,
upon which the economy is entirely dependent. In fact, more than
half of the developing countries (53%) have macroproject portfolios
that involve the development of two or more resources in their
country, whether extraction or processing project industries, and in
most cases this is in addition to infrastructure development (Figure
2.3) Such macroprojects that are part of multifaceted portfolios by
developing countries account for 85 percent of all projects and 93
percent of all capital investment. In contrast, only one-third of the

Figure 2.3

Distribution of Macroprojects
By Host Country Portfolio Composition

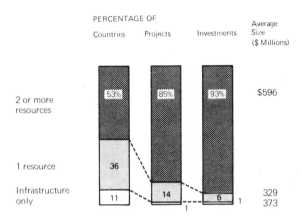

PERCENTAGE OF

Countries   Projects   Investments   Average Size ($ Millions)

2 or more resources   53%   85%   93% $596

1 resource   36

Infrastructure only   11   14   6   329 / 373

countries have projects developing a single resource or project industry sector, and their projects are fewer in number, and smaller in average investment size. Finally, only one-tenth of the countries have macroprojects only in the infrastructure sector. These are smaller ($379 million on average) and are typically projects for which they would be able to marshall financial support from international and regional development banks, such as the World Bank.

It appears that high industrial investment in the early 1970s might have sparked the high infrastructural investment in the later part of the decade, based on observations on the industrial/infrastructure breakdown throughout the 1970s (Figure 2.4). There seems to be a cyclical relationship. In fact, industrial initiatives might well create the need for, as well as generate the capital for, increased infrastructural initiatives.

Most Active Countries

A close examination of the top twenty host countries responsible for the bulk of total macroproject activity (67 percent of the total number of projects; 78 percent of the total investment) confirms these findings (Figure 2.5). The major common feature of

Figure 2.4

Industry versus Infrastructure Development Projects: Breakdown of New Announcements (Percentage)

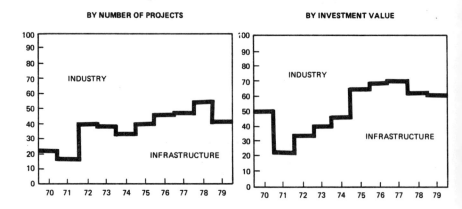

these 20 countries is that three-quarters of these most active countries have oil reserves and are net oil-exporters.

There are several notable features of these major host country macroproject customers:

1. Most of these countries have medium to high per capita incomes: 35 percent have per capita incomes of more than $2000; 55 percent, $500 to $1999. Only Egypt ($480), India ($190) and Indonesia ($370) have per capita incomes of less than $500 (Egypt and Indonesia are oil exporters; India has a large local market).

2. Ninety percent of these countries are sponsoring macroprojects across the board in hydrocarbon processing, metals, other manufacturing, and infrastructure. On an individual project industry basis, they have projects in every project industry sector.

3. Although the host countries are largely net oil exporters, surprisingly hydrocarbon processing has a relatively low share of the total investment portfolio of these top countries. This supports the earlier observation that oil dollars are in fact being channelled into other sectors of the economy in these countries.

Figure 2.5

Top Twenty Host Countries:
Mix of Projects by Industry and Host Organization

INVEST-MENT (Billions of Dollars)	NO. OF PROJECT	AVERAGE SIZE PER PROJECT (Millions of Dollars)	HOST COUNTRY	PROJECT INDUSTRY				ORGANIZATION		
				Hydrocarbon Processing	Metals	Other Industries	Infrastructure	Parastatal Corporation	Local Company	Government Ministries
$150.1	121	$1,240	Saudi Arabia	16%	3%	3%	78%	19%	29%	52%
119.6	108	1,108	Iran	30	7	9	54	47	21	32
83.2	106	785	Brazil	25	33	15	27	35	60	5
43.7	56	781	Egypt	18	9	11	62	17	24	59
38.7	69	561	Algeria	36	7	33	23	62	19	19
37.5	82	457	Australia	21	59	7	13	2	91	7
37.0	52	712	Iraq	33	2	17	48	85	0	15
34.8	45	774	South Korea	24	11	16	49	3	81	16
31.6	81	390	India	48	21	7	24	32	56	12
27.4	27	1,014	Venezuela	33	41	7	19	35	46	19
26.2	37	708	Turkey	57	11	8	24	5	72	23
26.0	59	441	Mexico	46	17	12	25	35	47	18
25.1	43	585	Argentina	44	16	14	26	29	41	29
15.3	24	637	Thailand	21	4	8	67	40	14	46
14.4	19	760	Nigeria	26	11	16	47	32	21	47
14.4	44	328	Indonesia	41	18	16	25	28	44	28
14.3	26	549	Malaysia	27	19	4	50	43	38	19
13.5	41	329	Philippines	12	37	14	37	9	57	33
11.2	13	861	Hong Kong	8	0	0	92	13	61	26
10.8	27	400	Kuwait	18	0	4	78	6	41	53

*Portfolio totals include projects in all stages from planning to start - up and currently postponed.

4. Some of these top countries put their largest concentration of investment effort into infrastructure — these include Saudi Arabia, Thailand, Hong Kong, and Kuwait. Saudi Arabia and Kuwait made giant leaps forward in development in the 1970s due to their sudden oil wealth. A large portion of the portfolios provided the urban infrastructure to support their industrial expansion — airports, housing, hospitals, schools, universities, military bases, desalination plants, etc. Hong Kong's premier project was its mass transit system. With other projects it provides the base to support Hong Kong's manufacturing focus.

5.   On a country by country basis, the makeup of host
     participants varies.   Within the top twenty countries,
     newly oil-rich countries such as Iran and Algeria have a
     high parastatal presence, with at least half of these
     governmental firms involved in the oil industry.   For
     example, the National Iranian Oil Company has about 19
     projects under active consideration or underway, while
     Sonatrach (Algeria) has 17 projects in various stages of
     development.   Egypt is an example of a country with a
     high government administrative presence on macro-
     projects.   This is partially explained by the unusually high
     percentage of infrastructure projects underway — each
     supervised by the appropriate government ministry.

HOST BUYERS GAINING SOPHISTICATION

Host buyers have changed significantly over the last decade.
In many cases they have mandated the creation of multinational-
level parastatal and local corporations.   They have taken on the
management of a large number of projects alone, while at the same
time they have been willing to ask for assistance when necessary —
on their terms.   Further, there are signs that they are beginning to
manage their own growth conflicts in more constructive ways.

Local Corporate Entities Created

There are now important worldscale parastatal enterprises and
local corporations, as well as emerging engineering and construction
companies capable of marshalling appropriate levels of support for
these macroprojects — formed specifically by government mandate,
or targeted policy decisions, to develop an internal support base for
macroproject development activities.   Overall, the most significant
fact about host participation is that at least one local company or
institution has been found to be associated in some way with each
macroproject.

Some of the faster-growing countries (such as Brazil) and the
developed countries (i.e. Australia) have an industrial base of both
local resources and companies sophisticated enough to support
macroprojects.   A significant number of their local companies are
involved in initiating projects of this magnitude, among them Broken

Hill Proprietary and Comalco of Australia; Cia. Vale do Rio Doce, Petrobras, and Siderbras in Brazil. In the newly oil-rich countries, however, parastatal and government entities represent the only vehicle for local participation in macroprojects in their country.

Major host sponsors on macroprojects in the Third World have impressive portfolios in terms of sheer number of projects, as well as the number which they are sponsoring independently (Table 2.1). Sonatrach (Algeria) and Pemex (Mexico) have the largest number of projects overall, as well as the largest number independently owned. All the major host sponsors, with the exception of Comalco Products of Australia, are parastatal corporations.

Table 2.1

Major Host Sponsors: Portfolio Breakdown By Contract Type

Company Type	Company Name	Number of Projects	
		Sole Owner	Joint Venture
Oil Companies	Sonatrach, Algeria	25	1
	Natl. Iranian Oil Co.	16	4
	Pemex, Mexico	22	-
	Petromin, S. Arabia	5	6
	Pertamina, Indonesia	8	4
	Abu Dhabi National Oil	5	4
	Petrobras, Brazil	11	1
	Iraq National Oil	11	-
Petrochemical Companies	SABIC, Saudi Arabia	2	11
	Fertilizer Corp. of India	8	-
	Natl. Petrochemical of Iran	4	4
	Ofc. Cher. des Phos., Morocco	7	1
Metal Companies	Cia Vale do Rio Doce, Brazil	5	13
	Comalco Products, Australia	1	7
	Mineroperu, Peru	7	3

Parastatal corporations provide a stability to local business activities of a country by removing them from vulnerability to political turbulence and activities. Newly formed parastatal corporations are staffed with professionals who may even be hired from international corporations in the industry. The employees of parastatals often receive lifetime appointments and are offered career opportunities within the enterprise. Thus, a continuity is established which makes it less subject to any changes and turbulence in the local government. Further, divorcing the resource company from direct ties with the government gives it the potential to compete with international corporations in the global industry. An example of one such parastatal corporation is Saudi Arabia Basic Industries Corporation (SABIC). It is a government-owned corporation, recently formed to help implement the Kingdom's industrial development plans in such industries as petrochemicals, fertilizer, aluminum and steel. SABIC represents the government in joint venture partnerships such as the Sabic Pectin Company, a 50-50 joint venture with Shell to undertake a $1.6 billion ethylene project in Yanbu.

Local engineering/construction companies, among others, have been increasing in number and level of expertise. The host countries which lead in the number of macroprojects within their borders are also leaders in the number of design and construction contracts won by local companies. This suggests that macroprojects are instrumental in developing local expertise. Based on the level of development in their local technology, they vary in the extent to which they contribute to the design and construction — whether independent or as a part of a turnkey consortium (Figure 2.6A). Brazilian, Saudi Arabian and Iranian companies are most frequently partners in consortium, while Mexican engineers do a lot of preliminary design work; and South Korean and Indian companies most frequently win independent construction contracts. On the lower technology infrastructure projects, host contractors have quite a respectable share of total macroproject contracts (Figure 2.6B).

In addition to contracts won domestically, there are some local engineering/construction companies that also compete internationally. Examples include South Korea's Hyundai Construction Corporation ($944 million contract to expand the port at Jubail) and Pakistan's National Construction Company (lead participant of a

45

Figure 2.6

Host Locals and Parastatals:
Interface in Macroproject Construction

A. Major Host Participants: Portfolio Comparisons

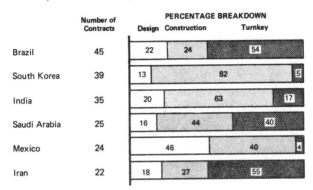

B. Overall Host Share of Infrastructure
   Project Contracts

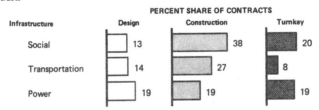

consortium of eight Brazilian construction companies to install a $248 million hydroelectric plant at Rio Negro, Uruguay).

Local content and local labor requirements have done much to promote the emergence of local capabilities. Although local manufacturers might not produce products that meet international quality standards in all cases, a local partner in a consortium would be able to identify these differences well in advance of the start-up of the completed installation. Local designers can provide easy and accurate knowledge of the local climatic and geological conditions. Local constructors can often suggest and work with such things as bamboo scaffolding, and other inexpensive approaches appropriate in a developing environment.

Willing To Go It Alone or Joint Venture

When countries with similar resource bases yet different stages of development are compared, quite different buying patterns and purchase decisions emerge.

Iran and Brazil, as examples, have similar resource bases of extensive petroleum reserves; macroproject commitments that are in various stages of development; and each has some development activity in other minerals. They differ with regard to their overall level of economic development, and their geographic location. They plan their development differently, and have distinctive expectations of what multinationals can contribute to their projects.

Iran was a model of extremely rapid industrial development during the 1970s. Newly rich from development of its oil resources, Iran had 108 macroprojects costing nearly $120 billion dollars in various stages of progress over the decade. More than half of these projects were committed to infrastructural development. The launching of highly sophisticated industrial projects taxed the internal pool of managerial and technical skills.

Several major parastatal corporations were formed to participate in joint ventures with international firms in oil, petrochemical and metal projects — such as the National Iranian Oil Company, the National Petrochemical Company, and the National Iranian Steel Company. For example, on the $1.2 billion Bandar Shahpur Petrochemical projects of 16 units, the National Iranian Oil Company represented Iranian interests in a joint venture with the Iran-Japan Petrochemical Company, a Japanese consortium that agreed to purchase 70 percent of the output under a long-term purchase agreement. Iran was able to handle some fertilizer and gas-gathering projects independently.

To generate momentum in infrastructure development, the assistance of foreign contractors was sought. A lot of progress was made possible by consortia of contractors, composed largely of European companies, who agreed to install complex facilities on a fixed-fee basis while assuming all financial and managerial risks. The consortia developed packages at the billion dollar level as well as for the smaller projects. Some examples are:

- A Franco-American consortium called Confraran (Jean Lefevre (France) and Morrison Knudson (U.S.) were lead participants) constructed a $2 billion highway from Teheran to the southern ports.

- An Italian consortium constructed two thermal power plants — one in Bandar Abbas ($160 million) and one in Esfahan ($150 million).
- A West German consortium of Huta Hagerfeld, Karl Schoen, and E. Hertkamp constructed a $120 million hydroelectric power station and tunnel.

Many of these participants responded to Iran's need to develop rapidly and packaged these bids quickly — but with numerous escalator clauses and margins for contingencies to protect themselves from the rampant inflation, clogged ports, etc.

Brazil, in contrast, has a very rich and fast-growing economy that has been at the development game for some time. Regarded as one of the more advanced developing countries, Brazil is clearly more seasoned than was Iran. Although Brazil's development achievements vary from region to region, and sector to sector, overall Brazilians are quite capable of undertaking macroprojects without outside assistance.

Nevertheless, there are situations and conditions under which international assistance is welcomed. In Brazil, the very largest macroprojects are developed by numerous Brazilian parastatal and local companies with some support and cooperation from multinational entities.

Petroleos Brasileiros (Petrobras) the parastatal petroleum company, has numerous projects in its portfolio that are being independently sponsored, while others are joint venture undertakings. Camacari in Bahia, a $3 billion complex of 22 petrochemical plants, is sponsored by a group of local petrochemical companies (such as Petrobras Quimica, Estirino or Nordeste, CPC Petroquimica, Polipropilene, S.A. and Fesiba) in joint venture with an array of international partners (such as Mitsubishi, ICI, Sumitomo Chemical, Badger, and Lummus).

Consortia of contractors are not typical in Brazil, with its highly developed local construction and manufacturing sectors. However, on the enormous $8 billion Itaipu Hydroelectric project (12,600 MW) in Parana State, a binational joint venture between the Brazilian and Paraguayan governments, the risks were so great and the scope so far beyond the capabilities of any individual company that a consortium of 10 construction companies was formed. It included 5 Brazilian and 5 Paraguayan companies. Also 85 percent of the materials was to be supplied by Brazilian manufacturers. The consortia they successfully competed against included: 1) A Canadian consortium with General Electric of Canada as lead participant; 2) A U.S. consortium with General Electric (U.S.) as lead; 3) A Japanese consortium with Hitachi as lead; and 4) a European consortium led by Siemens and Brown Boveri.

More Constructive in Resolving Conflicts

During the 1970s numerous crises emerged. The presence of crises is not really a surprise. More amazing is the great variety of tactics that were relied upon to resolve the conflict.

Conflicts over national goals manifested themselves in Iran and Mexico during the 1970s as the influx of oil-dollars redefined the level and scale of what they could realistically accomplish, and both governments pushed for maximum growth. The resolutions of their conflicts were quite different.

By 1977, rumors were spreading that Iran was developing too fast. Social change, and the resulting internal conflicts, was forcing people to lose their sense of direction as a nation. The Shah was pushing for rapid modernization, and more specifically, Westernization. The seeds for revolt that led to the deposition of the Shah in Februry 1979 were gestating.

In 1979 numerous projects were halted or abandoned for an indefinite period. Projects just months away from completion were deserted. Investments were in question. The Japanese were the first to renegotiate their contracts. They changed the name of their petrochemical complex from Bandar Shahpur to Bandar Khomeni and kept the project moving.

The key lesson more than any other is that culture must be respected and included in development or the very soul of the nation will take a "backlash." Backlash is defined as a return to a social consciousness even more traditional than the point at which the revolt occurred.

In the mid '70s in Mexico, the government communicated to the public that the country's new oil wealth would be used to benefit the general public. Billboards, radio announcements, and newspaper advertisements were used to inform the public that oil dollars were funding the new roads, highways, and other infrastructure projects essential to developing their country. Although the government may have been motivated by the fear of political unrest, whatever the motive, they fostered a sense of common direction.

Conflicts over industrial sector development objectives were witnessed in Brazil and Indonesia, both with sophisticated metal mining and processing sectors.

In some respects, Brazil's very strengths in the macroproject arena are leading to problems. Brazil is becoming increasingly demanding and rigid in negotiating its joint venture arrangements, resulting in pullouts by prospective partners or significant delays during negotiations. For example:

- On the $3.5 billion Carajas Iron Ore project, CVRD's pressure to diminish U.S. Steel's control during construction, compounded by its very stringent local ownership require-ments, provoked U.S. Steel to withdraw from the project and forced CVRD to scale down planned capacity and proceed alone.

- On the $2.1 billion Tubarao Steel project, Brazil was eager to raise the percentage of local products to be used in the construction of the plant. The Japanese proposed a maximum 30 to 33 percent local content, but the Brazilians requested 60 percent. The debate ended with 33 percent Brazilian content, but the project was delayed, resulting in the extension of the completion date by one year.

In the mineral sector, Indonesia relies more on international assistance, since the up-front capital needed to undertake mineral development projects has been generally beyond the means of the country to provide.

The Indonesia Ministry of Mines, which oversees all mineral development activity, is highly respected by the mining companies involved in projects in Indonesia because of its absolute honoring of the terms of project contracts. Projects in Indonesia are protected against unilateral changes by the system of "generations" of mineral agreements referred to above. Different sets of regulations are promulgated for contracts signed after different dates, each succeeding generation being somewhat more favorable to the host. Such regulations include:

- Deposit of a percentage of foreign exchange earnings from mining exports into a special account to be used for jointly agreed purposes

- Liability for a 10 percent export tax
- Duty-free import of equipment and materials allowed for the first 10 years of production
- A 20 percent capital expenditure deduction allowed from taxable income during the first 4 years of production (5 percent annually).

Their newest, third-generation legislation offers fewer incentives or benefits to outside investors, yet the terms are still fair and attractive because of the reliable reputation of the mining sector.

All of these efforts were undertaken by Third World governments to achieve specific purposes, namely, to rapidly industrialize; to evolve a local corporate infrastructure; and to develop sound purchase decisions.

In general, hosts are continually changing macroproject customers. Their needs are changing as their income and ability to purchase becomes enhanced. More specifically:

- The more developed the host, the more macroprojects it is likely to sponsor and the broader the range of projects
- The more developed the host, the more capable its local corporate infrastructure will be to sponsor, design, construct and supply a macroproject
- The more developed the host — as a country or within a particular industry — the more demanding the host will be in formulating terms of purchase.

3
Multinational as
Macroproject Supplier

The decision to compete in the macroproject arena is a complex and difficult one. The current list of major guest multinationals includes the very best companies that the industrialized nations have to offer. They have made their decision to compete for positions on macroprojects because of perceived host demand for a technology or expertise that they are particularly competent or skilled at providing. Potential participants are also aware of who they are competing against (other guest multinationals and local host companies who might be bidding for the job, or negotiating equity), and have determined that they have a clear competitive advantage and will be able to execute the job successfully. Since multinationals can compete along different cost and/or quality dimensions, what one competitor considers an advantage might be insignificant or irrelevant to the others.

The competitive arena in the Third World has been a constantly changing one for multinationals. During the past decade, numerous shifts in demand — and reputation — have occurred. Early in the decade, multinationals, as a group, had the image that they operated in a developing country as if they owned the place, or as if they were so powerful, or so entrenched, that the needs of the host countries were irrelevant. Multinationals were often characterized as raping the host country, despoiling its resources, and repatriating all of the profits and benefits for themselves. They could not declare themselves above reproach, as detailed accounts of their exploitation and abusive use of power had been factually documented by numerous researchers during the 1960s and early 1970s.

The sudden surge of capital transferred to oil-producing countries by the oil embargo, as well as that additional capital made available to developing countries on a short-term loan basis, for the first time, by private international banking institutions, instigated the flood of new projects proposed during the mid-1970s. Assistance was required — even urgently demanded — of international engineering/construction firms, and equipment manufacturers, while multinational oil companies, as an example, were being pressured by existing events to diversify either their sources of supply or their basic business activities. Their management expertise and access to international markets was welcome; their equity in local facilities was not.

Regardless of the exceptionally high, and enthusiastic, demand for multinationals' services and goods, the implementation of these projects did not go smoothly. During the course of the field interviews for this macroproject survey, irate customers with considerable hostility toward their multinational suppliers could, indeed, be found. Upon closer analysis, however, their difficulties could be attributed more to the extremely unsatisfactory contracts and working relationships that they agreed to when initiating their projects than to any deliberate contractual violations by multinational guests. (It should be noted, of course, that there were also customers who were considerably enriched by such transnational collaborations.)

By the end of the decade new project announcements tapered off, as it was becoming increasingly evident that over-capacity and/or debt repayment problems might exist. Multinational corporations found themselves in increasingly stronger competition with each other in trying to win in the smaller pool of investment or service contracts on newly launched macroprojects. They were being more rigorously evaluated and compared to each other on the basis of the quality and cost features of their proposals. The more successful multinationals within the macroproject arena have distinguished themselves by being able to expertly tailor their participation in the Third World to needs of specific customer groups and their unique project requirements. At the same time, most host enterprises had become enlightened about the fact that it is the contractual negotiations with multinational guests that can doom or make a macroproject. When their services are properly negotiated and contracted for, multinationals can be depended upon to provide genuine mentoring of host organizations and staff in managerial and technological systems and methods, not to mention the capital, equipment and access to world markets they can make available.

This chapter focuses on the competitive strategies of the leading guest multinationals including their expertise in segmenting the macroproject market into meaningful customer clusters; their ability to tailor their services to specific customer needs; their competence at marshalling global professional talent, capital goods and technology to fulfill project requirements in the most efficient manner; and their skill in designing exclusive technologies or fixed cost packages that offer important quality or cost advantages to the macroproject customer. The forms of collaboration that have emerged will be discussed in Chapters 4 and 5.

SOUND MARKET SEGMENTATION CRITICAL

A potential supplier of services or goods must be aware of what the customer wants and who the customer is in order to make the best offer. Suppliers can define precisely who their best customers are likely to be by dividing the sample of macroproject customers into segments or clusters according to certain features or characteristics determined to be indicative of a need for a specific service. The more accurate the features selected are as indicators of customer demand or buying habits, the more skillful the segmentation will be, and the more mileage the supplier will ultimately be able to derive from the technology he has developed; the licenses he holds; and the marketing network and efforts his commits to scouting for macroproject business opportunities in the Third World.

Multinationals might segment the macroproject arena by such customer features as 1) level of economic development or income (oil-exporters, newly industrialized, resource-rich developing, Poor-I, Poor-II, Poor-III); 2) geographic location (Middle East/North Africa, Latin America, Asia, Sub-Saharan Africa); or 3) project industry being developed (oil refineries, petrochemical plants, electric power or transportation systems, etc.; or high technology, low technology, etc.).

The supplier relies on customer demand information to determine the optimum way to organize the marketing effort to reach the right customer groups with the best services or goods offer. Clustering customers by per capita income level would surface opportunities to achieve marketing efficiencies. Suppliers with broad lines of services or goods to offer would be more likely to focus on those medium- or high-income developing countries who have very broad-based and diverse portfolios of macroprojects underway within their borders. A supplier who is competent in many industrial and infrastructural areas might consider opening an office or forming joint ventures with local companies within these more active countries, as deeper knowledge of local procedures and key people in the industry can optimize the number of bids won.

Grouping customers along geographic lines would facilitate identification of logistical and procurement efficiencies (i.e., buying goods in bulk to be shipped to several projects in the same region) as well as any efficiencies that can be derived from cultural and language similarities and travel proximities.

In contrast, if a very specific technology is to be marketed, segmentation of customers by the project industry they wish to develop, regardless of their level of economic development or geographic location, would be the most meaningful way to determine demand and organize the marketing effort.

The typical supplier will segment the customer base according to the interrelationship of multiple variables, as each cut yields a different profile of customer needs. Multinational management then has the choice of meeting customer demand by making available a full line of services or products across many project industry sectors, or by covering the world in a selective way. Within the macroproject arena, numerous perspectives on the optimum way to market services and goods can be found.

Marketing Spans the Globe

Most multinational macroproject participants market their goods and services throughout the developing world. A geographic distribution of all OECD-six participants' contracts shows some interesting patterns of mix and concentration (Figure 3.1). Each major OECD country has contractual obligations underway in all four host regions, even in high-risk and low per-capita-income Sub-

Figure 3.1

Profile of International Participant Mix by Host Region
(Weighted Participation)*

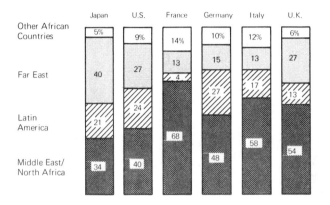

Saharan Africa. All but one of the major OECD-six have won most of their contracts in the Middle East/North Africa region during the 1970s, which, because of oil dollars and oil supply, was the area with the largest concentration of projects and the highest incentives for participation. Japan is an exception, as it had most of its contracts underway in neighboring countries in the Far East, since there are efficiencies associated with doing business with geographically proximate countries.

Political Ties Important

Political linkages influence purchase decisions and therefore need to be taken into account when developing a marketing strategy. Since many countries have portfolios of only one project or between one and three projects, purchases are made on an ad-hoc basis, and no indications of supplier loyalties are discernible. Some of the host countries with larger portfolios, such as Iran, have awarded contracts to guest multinationals from all OECD-six nations to an appreciable extent (Figure 3.2). Other countries with major project portfolios appear to have more skewed selection patterns. Saudi Arabia is such an example: The U.S., more than any other country, holds the dominant share of macroproject contracts.

Figure 3.2

Profile of International Participant Mix for Selected Countries (Weighted Participation)*

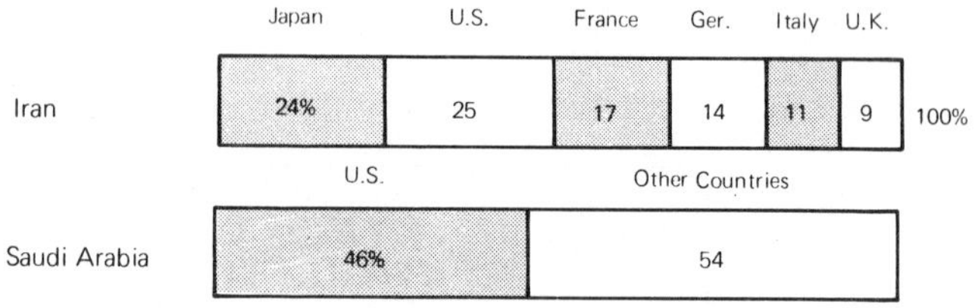

* Equivalent to the total number of contracts to which the participants are committed, rather than actual number of participants.

When a particular guest nationality plays a more prominent role in developing the macroprojects of a certain host country, as is the case in Saudi Arabia, some intergovernmental commitment to that host country's development is usually indicated. These ties can be based on a long history of collaboration between the two countries; the countries might be geographic neighbors; the host country might have been a colony of the industrialized country; or there might be some industry compatability. For example, many of the largest projects going on in Brazil in partnership with the Japanese are the result of the (resource-rich) Brazilian government's direct request for (resource-poor) Japanese participation and support. The close diplomatic relations between the United States and Mexico or Venezuela, as valued neighbors, and Saudia Arabia, as a long-term supplier of crude oil to the U.S., would create a situation where U.S. companies would feel more familiar with the way things are done in those countries, thus providing an inducement to U.S. companies to focus their best efforts on winning contracts and proposals within those borders. Sound intergovernmental relations provide the net result of enhancing the comfort-level among prospective partners from two countries. In many instances, the political aspects of intergovernmental relations can outweigh business considerations.

Project Industries Transnational

Each project industry sector has unique customer requirements that are best addressed on a worldwide basis. The Third World market for petrochemical macroprojects, for example, is a 109-project market worth $53 billion, underway in twenty-eight host

Table 3.1

Third World Market for Macroproject-Scale Petrochemical Facilities

		No. of Projects	Investment ($MM)
Middle East/North Africa			
Abu Dhabi	SO	1	300
Algeria	SO	5	1,225
Egypt	SO+JV	3	1,500
Iran	SO-JV	9	3,713
Iraq		2	3,700
Kuwait	JV	3	2,700
Libya	SO	2	900
Morocco	SO	4	830
Qatar	JV	1	500
Saudi Arabia	JV	8	6,078
Turkey	SO+JV	3	1,985
		41	23,431
Latin America			
Argentina	SO+JV	9	3,066
Bolivia	SO+JV	2	1,147
Brazil	SO+JV	11	5,830
Chile	JV	2	450
Ecuador	JV	1	1,500
Mexico	SO	7	2,000
Puerto Rico	JV	1	300
Venezuela	SO+JV	2	930
		35	15,223
Far East			
Australia	JV	6	2,080
India	SO	8	3,582
Indonesia	JV	4	1,800
New Zealand	JV	1	500
Philippines	JV	1	800
Singapore		2	1,176
South Korea	SO+JV	5	3,607
Taiwan	SO+JV	5	874
Thailand	JV	1	400
		33	14,819
Total		109	53,473

JV — Joint venture
SO — Sole owner

Table 3.2

Multinationals With Equity Participation In Third World Petrochemical Macroprojects

Company Type	Breakdown of Multinational Corporations by Country of Origin		
	United States	Japan	W Ger, UK, Italy, France
Petrochemical/ Chemical	Celanese Diamond Shamrock Dow Chemical Dupont Hercules Union Carbide W.R. Grace Chemtex Fibres Monsanto Oxirane Corp. Texas Eastern Bordon Chemical	Asahi Chem. Kuraray Mitsubishi Mitsui Pehem. Mitsui Toatsu Nippon Chem. Sumitomo Chem. Toyo Soda Mfg.	Hoechst (W. Ger.) ICI (U.K.) Montecatini Edison (Italy) CDF Chimie (France) Technimont (Italy) Esso Chemie (U.K.)
Oil	Amoco Oil Exxon Mobil Georgia-Pacific Houston National Gas	Kyowa Gas	Shell
Trading	Cleveland Cliffs Hatco Group	C. Itoh Marubeni Mitsubishi Mitsui Nichimen Nissho Iwai	

countries of varying local market sizes (Table 3.1). On a regional basis, these macroprojects are distributed about equally among the Middle East/North Africa, Latin America and the Far East; however, no projects of this dimension have been proposed in the Sub-Saharan African countries, due to their dearth of oil resources. The projects in the Middle East/North Africa are larger on average than those underway in the other regions. The total planned capacity additions of those petrocheical projects proposed during the 1970s included more than 12 million tons-per-year of ethylene; 4 million tpy methanol; 3 million tpy chlorine/caustic soda; as well as various quantities of derivatives such as propylene, ethylene dichloride, benzene and polyethylene. Many of the petrochemicals further downstream are not specifically mentioned here as they do not independently require a capital investment of more than $100 million, although they might be a downstream unit of one of the larger petrochemical complexes in the macroproject sample.

Most countries participating in this industry have more than one project on the drawing boards and most of the host organizations sponsoring these projects have been willing to joint venture when necessary to promote these value-adding projects. More than 85 host corporations in total are involved in sponsoring these projects — although only slightly more than ten of these are sponsors of multiple projects (i.e., SABIC, 9; Iranian Oil Co, 8; Pemex, 6; etc.). Thus the actual list of prospective buyers is long and very diverse.

In addition to petrochemical companies, new players became interested in participating in petrochemical macroprojects during the 1970s: Oil companies integrated forward into petrochemicals from their basic oil exploration and production activities, while trading companies, attracted by the opportunity to purchase the output, stepped up their involvement in the largest projects underway. Table 3.2 lists the sponsoring multinational participants by name. U.S. and Japanese companies dominate, with U.S. petrochemical and oil companies vying for equity on these projects against other Japanese and European petrochemical companies and Japanese trading companies. When one considers that $53 billion in petrochemical projects is being invested, in fact the list seems small. In addition, these companies are involved to a very limited extent — they have but one project per participant. Thus not only are the projects and host sponsors diverse, but the multinationals collaborating in joint ventures are diverse, creating a situation of relatively little accumulation of experience in transnational collaboration on either side. The supplier, in fact, seems to initiate only about one major project per decade, but must, nevertheless, be aware of any moves his competitors are making.

MORE SUCCESSFUL SUPPLIERS TAILOR SERVICES

As suppliers vary the breadth and depth of their expertise (i.e., they may participate in more than one project industry sector such as petrochemicals and metals; or they may provide more than one unique process such as ammonia and urea), their target customers and list of competitors will expand or contract. Thus, it is very important that the supplier define his line of service and expertise in a very clear way. The more limited the range of services or goods offered the more targeted and focused the supplier must be in preparing his proposal.

The portfolios of contracts won by the leading companies suggest that a very broad-based range of services coupled with some specific technological or management expertise or focus may be the key components of a winning strategy. Multinational participants can learn a great deal about Third World macroproject customer needs by observing the contractual approaches and range of services provided by their competitors.

Suppliers Have Diverse Specialties

Some companies focus on satisfying a particular project requirement more than others (Table 3.3). Overall, U.S. resource companies make their major contributions by providing equity capital while the Japanese, Italian and West German resource companies are more willing to transfer technology on a contractual basis with separate long-term purchase contracts. In contrast, the Japanese trading companies participate in both equity and technology transfer capacities. U.S. and U.K. firms are the leading providers of independent design and consulting assistance to project owners.

Competitors can be broken down into project industry subsegments. Some companies of certain OECD-six nationalities have greater competitive prominence in certain industry sectors, more than others: companies from the U.S. outnumber other nationalities among oil/gas, engineering/construction, and telecommunications companies; while the Japanese are most prominent among petrochemical, metal, pulp and paper, and trading companies; and the West Germans head the list among equipment manufacturers.

Any Supplier Can Adapt

The range of contracts awarded to multinational guests during the 1970s showed that guest companies, regardless of type, were enormously resilient and flexible in meeting the requirements of macroprojects. The successful multinationals seemed to win on their ability to add value beyond what had been traditionally expected of them on smaller projects or within different business environments. Every type of participant company has been found to meet any and all project requirements when necessary (i.e. equity capital; technology transfer including design and construction; and market access, whether production-sharing or long-term purchase) (also Table 3.3). Resource companies (oil/gas, petrochemical, aluminum, steel or other metals, and pulp and paper) have been found to provide design and/or construction (including project management) services on a fairly frequent basis. Thus, in addition to their pursuit of access to the host country's raw materials, they also compete in the macroproject arena on a technology level. Engineering/construction firms, on the other hand, have been found to take on equity share in macroprojects, or to market the output of a plant under a countertrade arrangement under certain very specific circumstances.

1. The major multinational sponsors often provide design, construction and project-management services, in addition to their participation as joint venture partners (Table 3.4). The leading companies include Royal Dutch Shell of U.K./Netherlands; Mitsui Toatsu, Sumitomo Chemical, Nippon Steel and Kobe Steel, all of Japan; and Mobil Oil and Reynolds of U.S. origin; among others. They take on these broad-based responsibilities in developing oil refinery, LNG, petrochemical, aluminum and steel projects for the most part.

2. The major engineering/construction companies provide project management expertise in addition to design and construction services. Among the top ten engineering/

Table 3.3

Breakdown of Contracts Per Company Type For Major Guest Participant Nationalities

Company Type	Major Participant Nationality	Number of		Capital Sourcing (Equity)	Technology Transfer		Market Access	
		Cos.	Cntrs.		Design*	Constr.*	Production Sharing	Long-Term Purchase
				Percent Distribution				
Oil/Gas	1. U.S.	36	77	77	10	13	X	X
	2. U.K.	8	32	57	9	34	X	X
	3. Japan	15	26	24	38	38	X	X
Petrochem	1. Japan	20	45	58	29	13		X
	2. U.S.	31	40	48	30	23	X	X
	3. Italy	7	27	26	30	44		X
Aluminum	1. Japan	8	20	50	20	30		X
	2. U.S.	9	17	88	6	6		
Steel	1. Japan	12	43	63	9	28		
	2. W. Germany	11	28	14	14	72		X
	3. U.S.	10	11	70	10	30		
Other Metals	1. Japan	19	50	78	2	20	X	X
	2. U.S.	16	44	91	7	2		X
Pulp & Paper	1. Japan	13	21	100				

Company Type	Major Participant Nationality	Number of Cos.	Number of Cntrs.	Capital Sourcing (Equity)	Technology Transfer Design*	Technology Transfer Constr.*	Market Access Production Sharing	Market Access Long-Term Purchase
				Percent Distribution	Percent Distribution			
Trading	1. Japan	16	133	45	8	47		X
Engineer/ Construction	1. U.S.	150	376	1	40	59		
	2. U.K.	68	121	7	43	50		
	3. W. Germany	47	92	3	19	78		
	4. France	48	81	6	23	70		
	5. Italy	32	81	4	15	81		X
	6. Japan	38	80	1	13	86		X
Equip. Mfg. Elect.	1. W. Germany	19	64	2	16	83		
	2. Japan	10	34	3	6	91		X
	3. U.S.	18	27	19	11	70		
Equip. Mfg. Non-Electr.	1. W. Germany	9	39	3	5	92		
	2. Japan	17	31		3	97		
	3. U.S.	9	27	18		82		X
Communic.	1. U.S.	12	18		17	83		

Table 3.4

Major Guest Sponsors and Macroproject Portfolios

Type of Company	Name of Guest Sponsor	Number of Projects		Design/Construct
		Sole Owner	Joint Venture	
Oil Companies	Royal Dutch Shell, U.K./Neth.	2	15	X
	Mobil Oil, U.S.	–	4	
Petrochemical Companies	Mitsui Toatsu Chemical, Japan	–	5	X
	Montecatini-Edison, Italy	–	4	X
	Sumitomo Chemical, Japan	–	6	X
	ICI, U.K.	2		X
Metal Companies	Nippon Steel, Japan		2	X
	Kobe Steel, Japan		8	X
	Reynolds, U.S.	1	7	X
	Alusuisse, Switzerland		4	X
	Krupp Huttenwerke, W. Ger.		1	X
	Billiton Aluminum, Netherlands		7	X

construction services.   Among the top ten engineering/
construction companies active in the macroproject arena,
four are U.S. design/constructors (Pullman Kellogg, Bechtel, Fluor, and Foster Wheeler).   The remaining companies
have specific process technologies which they market in
turnkey or consortia packages which include design and
management.   These include: Toyo and Chiyoda (Japan),
Snamprogetti (Italy), Uhde (West Germany), and Lummus
(US/UK) (Table 3.5). Hyundai of South Korea, also among
the top ten companies, has its expertise concentrated in
the construction of major civil works.   All of these
companies have won both design and construction contracts, most have participated in consortia and held
project management contracts.   Few have conducted
feasibility studies or have provided only licensed process
technolgy without the construction component.

There are, of course, numerous types of specialty
companies involved in macroproject development, such as
consulting engineers, design engineers, constructors, and
general contractors.   The first two types are usually
responsible for the early stages of projects — feasibility,
process design and, for design engineers, basic and
detailed engineering and procurement.   Their work is
implemented by general construction firms who construct
and startup the project. Design/constructors, in contrast,
design, construct and manage all stages of these projects.
They are a U.S. phenomenon, and include such major
companies as Bechtel, Fluor, Badger, Parsons, Foster
Wheeler, Pullman Kellogg, McKee, and Brown and Root.
The leading companies are willing to participate on a
whole or partial basis, as the needs of the hosts require.
Bechtel exemplifies this.   Although Bechtel is most
typically involved in the capacity of design/constructor
(including project management) for some of the largest
projects in existence (for example, the $9 billion Al Jubail
Petrochemical City in Saudi Arabia, the $1.2 billion Badak
and Arun LNG projects in Indonesia, and the $1.1 billion
LNG project in Shuiba, Kuwait), Bechtel has also done
feasibility studies (such as for a $300 million nickel

Table 3.5

Major Engineering/Construction Companies: Portfolios of Services to Macroprojects

Rank (By Ave. Size Project)	Rank (By Number of Contracts)	Company	Technology Transfer						
			Feasibility	Consult./Tech. Asst.	Design	Prov. Proc. Tech.	Contractor	Ctr./Consortium	Project Manager
7	1	Pullman, Kellogg, United States		X			X	X	X
8	2	Snam Progetti, Italy		X	X	X	X	X	X
2	3	Bechtel, United States	X	X			X	X	X
3	4	Fluor Constr. & Eng., United States	X	X			X	X	X
10	5	Uhde, Friedrich, West Germany			X	X	X	X	X
9	6	Toyo Engineering, Japan		X	X		X		X
5	7	Chiyoda Chem. Eng./Constr., Japan		X			X	X	
4	8	Hyundai Constr., South Korea		X	X		X		
6	9	Lummus, C.E., United Kingdom				X	X	X	X
1	10	Foster Wheeler, United States	X	X			X	X	X

project in Cerro Matoso, Colombia), and has functioned as a turnkey contractor for a specific segment of a project (i.e., the gas and truck lines of the $16 billion Saudi gas gathering system).

3. The major equipment manufacturers provide design and installation in addition to the capital equipment. In addition to equipment export, they often also construct the facility, either alone, or in consortium, under a 'plant export' or turnkey arrangement. Most of these companies also have held project management responsibility on such packages. They do not typically win independent design contracts, as the equipment and plant are already designed for plant export in their equipment sales package. These leading companies (Table 3.6) include the major electrical power systems providers: Brown Boveri (Switzerland), General Electric (U.S.), Kraftwerk Union (West Germany), Mitsubishi Heavy (including desalination technology, Japan), Siemens (West Germany), and Westinghouse Electric (U.S.). Lurgi and Klockner-Humbolt Deutz (West Germany), as well as Mitsubishi Heavy (Japan), won contracts for their petrochemical and other hydrocarbon processing technologies. Ishikawajima Harima won many contracts for its oil refinery expertise, and Topsoe (Denmark) provides an outstanding ammonia process for fertilizer projects.

Individual or independent contracts for equipment supply are generally minor in size when compared to these turnkey contracts. Examples from the project portfolio of Brown Boveri, a Swiss equipment manufacturer, will demonstrate this: Within Iran, Brown Boveri had a $125 million contract for plant and equipment for the Iran electricity system; a 36 percent share of a Swiss-West Germany consortium to build a gas- and coal-fired power station; a $13.4 million contract to supply equipment (gas turbines and transformers) for a switching station; and a $11.4 million contract to supply 21 electricity substations. These numerous alternative modes of scoping contracts demonstrates the need for multinational suppliers to be aware of and to

Table 3.6

Major Equipment Manufacturers: Portfolios of Services to Macroprojects

| Rank | | Company | Technology Transfer | | | | | | |
By Ave. Size Project	By Number of Contracts		Feasibility	Consult./Tech. Asst.	Design	Prov. Proc. Tech.	Contractor	Ctr./Consortium	Project Manager
2	1	Mitsubishi Heavy Ind., Japan	X				X	X	X
9	2	Lurgi Chem. & Hutten Tech., W. Ger.				X	X	X	
3	3	Ishikawajima Harima, Japan					X	X	X
1	4	Kraftwerk Union, West Germany		X			X	X	X
8	5	Klockner–Humbolt Deutz, West Germany					X	X	X
4	6	Siemens, West Germany		X			X	X	X
5	7	Brown, Boveri, Switzerland					X	X	X
10	8	Topsoe, Denmark					X	X	X
7	9	General Electric, United States					X	X	X
6	10	Westinghouse Electric, United States		X			X	X	X

employ varied strategies and tactics to meet the diverse and changing needs of Third World macroproject developers. The main observation that emerges from this examination of actual services provided is that the leading companies offer a full line of services to host macroprojects and are willing to participate under a variety of contractual arrangements. It falls to the host to negotiate the appropriate terms to ensure that the project is carried out in the best way.

GLOBAL MANAGEMENT A POWERFUL ADVANTAGE

It appears that the more global the multinational, the greater the economies of scale it can derive from global purchasing of capital goods, logistical coordination of professional services, imports, exports, and its marketing network. It is also able to more effectively build an internationally credible reputation. There can, of course, be local impediments to the smooth performance of a multinational at the global level, such as requirements for locally manufactured goods or use of local labor, tarriff barriers, customs restrictions. Nevertheless, for a multinational seeking to serve potential host customers in the most flexible and responsive way, not competing on a global level can, in fact, create a serious competitive disadvantage.

Sponsors Enable Forward/Backward Integration

Royal Dutch Shell, the leading multinational sponsor in the Third World, managed to survive the decade by maintaining, and even expanding its investment activities in the Third World. While major oil companies around the world experienced the 1970s as a very turbulent period of sudden nationalizations; significant reductions in their rights to equity; and threats to their supply sources; Shell kept a steady stream of investment projects in progress. Two of a total of 18 projects were in the planning stage; five were in negotiation; two, contract let; three, under construction; and three were completed by the end of 1979. An additional three were suspended for various reasons during the decade.

Shell has an impressive list of macroproject activities which reflects the global commitment to participation in the Third World which it has been sustaining for some time. (Table 3.7). Shell has

Table 3.7

Royal Dutch Shell: Portfolio of Third World Macroprojects

1. Oil Refineries

$ Million	Name/Location	Equity	% Cost Overrun	Years Delayed	Status
230	Abadan Lub Oil, Iran		–	–	Negotiation
830	Port Dickson, Malaysia	49%	–	–	Suspended
115	Si Racha, Thailand		–	–	Plan
1,000	Jubail, Saudi Arabia	50	–	–	Negotiation
400	Pulau Bukom, Singapore	100	–	–	Completed
4,700	Lantao Oil/Pchem, Hong Kong		–	–	Suspended
100	Dumai, Indonesia		–	–	Plan

2. LNG/LPG Plants

$ Million	Name/Location	Equity	% Cost Overrun	Years Delayed	Status
3,300	Northwest Shelf, Australia	17%	25%	6	Construction
210	Lumut LNG, Brunei	45	98	2	Completed
1,600	Ruweis Gas Gath/LPG, Abu Dhabi	15	33	1	Contract Let
1,000	Bintulu LNG, Malaysia	18	–	2	Negotiation
1,300	Maui LNG, New Zealand	20	–	1	Construction
2,500	Bonny LNG, Nigeria	12	–	–	Negotiation
350	Umm Saad LNG, Qatar	40	75	1	Construction
1,100	Shuaiba LPG, Kuwait	long-term purchase	10	–	Completed

3. Petrochemical Plants

$ Million	Name/Location	Equity	% Cost Overrun	Years Delayed	Status
130	Capuava Polypropylene, Brazil	47%	–	–	Completed
400	Bang Phra Chem, Thailand	50	33%	2	Contract Let
2,058	Al Jubail Pchem, Saudi Arabia		29	4	Negotiation

commitments to projects in fourteen countries throughout the developing world, including the Middle East, Asia, Oceania, Latin America and Africa — with Malaysia, Saudi Arabia and Thailand even meriting two investments per country. Shell is able to move into any country around the world with a sophisticated view of how things operate, and has the network to move goods and professional staff with ease.

Shell appears to be working with host sponsors in achieving forward integration. In addition to oil exploration (not included in the macroproject sample), and its basic business in oil refinery development (7 projects, $7.4 billion total investment), Shell has expanded activities by investing in LNG/LPG (8 projects, $11.4 billion), and petrochemical plant construction (3 projects, $2.5 billion) in joint ventures with host parastatal corporations.

Shell adjusted its equity requirements during the 1970s. Its equity position varied by type of project: Shell held 49% or more in equity in oil refinery projects; less than 45% equity in LNG/LPG projects; and about 50% equity in petrochemical facility projects. Over the course of the decade, Shell was required to reduce its equity expectations, as were other multinational oil companies: On the Lumut LNG project in Brunei, Shell and Mitsubishi enjoyed a 45 percent equity position each, with the Brunei government retaining 10 percent. In contrast, on their most recent project at Sarawak, Malaysia, Shell and Mitsubishi were only permitted to acquire 17 percent equity each, while Petronas (Malaysia) held the remaining 66 percent. Although offering less equity, Petronas was able to benefit from Shell's previous experience in designing and managing a similar project in another location. Shell was compensated for its services on a fee basis.

Design/Constructors Enable Scale Economies

The major engineering/construction companies managed to achieve a preeminent position in macroproject development by exhibiting a competence across a broad line of technologies (Table 3.8). Bechtel and Fluor of the U.S. have the broadest project industry expertise, with contracts underway in most hydrocarbon processing areas including oil refineries, LNG/gas processing, petrochemical, pipelines, as well as metal mining and processing. They are also competent in developing enormous infrastructure projects,

Table 3.8

Major Engineering/Construction Companies: Macroproject Portfolios by Project Industry Sector

Engineering/ Construction Company	Macroproject Industry Sector (Number of Contracts)						
	Oil Refining	LNG/Gas Processing	Petro-chemical	Fertilizer	Pipeline	Metal Mining	Metal Processing
Pullman Kellogg, U.S.	13	5	1	26			
Snamprogetti, Italy	10	2	3	10	6		
Bechtel, U.S.	2	5	2	1	5	4	8
Fluor, U.S.	5	5	4	1	3	4	
Uhde, W. Germany		1	7	17			
Toyo Eng., Japan		1	3	18			
Chiyodo, Japan	6	6	6	2			
Lummus, C.E., US/UK	2		13	1	1		
Foster Wheeler, U.S.	6		5	3	1		

including power, marine, and public facilities. The remaining companies have contracts in many project industry sectors, but dominate in one technological process area: Pullman Kellogg and Snamprogetti have won many contracts to install oil refineries and fertilizer plants; and both have competed with Uhde and Toyo Engineering in the fertilizer plant sector. Pullman Kellogg and Uhde have strong reputations for their ammonia process technologies, while Snamprogetti and Toyo compete against each other with their urea technologies. Lummus achieved great success with unique ethylene technology.

Bechtel, Fluor, Pullman Kellogg, and Lummus, as an example, have certain similarities. All have offices around the world, and are dependent for well over half of their sales from foreign projects (in some years over the last decade that percent has even reached 90 to 95% for some companies). Their engineering and construction sales grew substantially during the 1970s (for example, sales grew by 27 percent for Fluor, and 12 percent for Pullman Kellogg).

They vary in several ways. Both Fluor and Bechtel hold project management responsibility for some of the largest projects around. Fluor is project manager on the $21 billion Saudi Arabia Gas Gathering System; Bechtel is project manager and master planner on the $9 billion Al Jubail Petrochemical City, also in Saudi Arabia, as examples). They do enter into technology-development joint ventures, on occasion, but their reputations are based upon their ability to coordinate, engineer and design highly complex systems, regardless of the technology needed. Among the reasons for their selection as suppliers, customers identify: previous experience in installing a similar process; flexibility in dealing with complexity; and their excellent computerized project control systems; as the decisive factors. They are able to evaluate and select from any number of leading technologies in preparing a proposal — this is in addition to their technological specialties, such as Bechtel's nuclear power expertise and Fluor's offshore strengths.

In contrast, Pullman Kellogg and Lummus enjoy strong reputations for their ammonia and ethylene technologies, respectively. Lummus' technology supports 51% of the world's ethylene capacity, and Pullman Kellogg's has 50 percent of the world's ammonia capacity. Lummus has project management responsibility for the ethylene unit at the Camacari Petrochemical Complex in Brazil (22

units in total) for example, however, this responsibility was awarded
to them because of their technological expertise rather than for any
special features of their corporate infrastructure or management
capability. The largest projects Pullman Kellogg has managed
include the $3 billion Arzew LNG project and the $1.3 billion
Skikda II LNG project, both in Algeria, for which they were selected
for their efficient catalytic cracker gas processing technology.
They have also managed close to half of the forty macroproject
contracts they hold in the Third World, the bulk of which are in the
fertilizer industry sector. The investment sizes of these projects
are smaller, however, averaging between $100 and 300 million.
Further, Pullman Kellogg's ammonia contract sales plummeted in
the middle of the decade as Topsoe introduced a state-of-the-art
ammonia technology with numerous new efficiencies. Kellogg was
able to maintain its market position towards the end of the decade
due to repeat purchases from long-standing customers (i.e. Mexico).
Nevertheless, Pullman Kellogg's success appears to be closely linked
to technology.

EXCLUSIVE TECHNOLOGY/COST A COMPETITIVE EDGE

When a supplier possesses a state-of-the-art technology, or can
offer a bid package at a guaranteed fixed cost, a very strong
competitive edge over other bid packages can result. The
technology provider who has made a breakthrough can spread
research and development costs over multiple projects that it is
assured of winning. The provider of a guaranteed fixed cost package
is able to maximize his profits — if the project goes well — as these
packages typically allow the supplier maximum control, and maximum foreign content.

Exclusive Technology Ensures Demand

There are multinational suppliers of technology to macroprojects who participate in a very focused and specific way. For
example, there are a limited number of multinationals who are
actively marketing their exclusive petrochemical processes in the
Third World (Table 3.9). Although there are nineteen such
companies, no process is being marketed by more than four
suppliers. In fact, most multinationals are marketing only a single

Table 3.9

Multinational Providers of Petrochemical Process Technology to Third World Macroprojects

Company Name	Process Technology													Total Technologies
	Ethylene	ld PE	hd PE	Poly-pro	Chlor	PVC	TPA	Pro-pyl	Ethane	Metha-nol	Styrene	Ethyl-ben-zene	Etha-nol	
Amoco Chemical							X							1
Arco Polymer		X												1
CDF Chimie		X												1
Costain Carbide Badger											X			1
Davy Powergas									X					1
Diamond Shamrock					X									1
Hercules				X										1
Hoechst/Uhde			X			X								2
KTI									X					1
Lummus	X					X		X						3
Mitsui Petrochem.			X	X										2
Mobil–Badger			X									X		2
Montedison		X		X		X								3
Natl. Distillers		X												1
Shell	X								X				X	3
Stone & Webster	X													1
Technimont				X										1
Technip–KTI	X													1
Uhde					X					X				2
Providers – Total:	4	4	3	4	2	3	1	1	3	1	1	1	1	

process. The maximum number of petrochemical technologies known to be marketed per company is three. The exclusivity of the process provides the competitive edge. Their heavy investment in research and development requires that these companies market their product worldwide. They are selected or rejected vis-a-vis other suppliers on the basis of the features and economics of the process they are offering. A state-of-the-art technology typically includes major breakthroughs in productivity, improved product quality and more efficient plant economics, thus guaranteeing that it will be the technology of choice.

Guaranteed Cost in High Demand

The packaging of design and construction services under turnkey or consortia contracts was common during the 1970s. Because of their fixed-fee arrangements, those packages typically undercut other competitors on a cost basis. When a breakdown is made among contractors by type of contract they participated in, some interesting patterns emerge (Figure 3.3):

- West German, Italian, French, and Japanese contractors make their major contributions on a turnkey basis.
- Of the turnkey contracts, the West Germans, Italians and Japanese most frequently participate via consortia.
- In contrast, the U.S. and U.K. companies competed more independently — particularly as consultants/designers — which represents a large proportion of their total contracts.

There are many nuances of these participant dynamics which will be explained in Chapters 4 and 5. At this point it is only important to note that these packages have very large foreign proportions of capital goods and services, and turn full project management responsibility over to the supplier. Further, they had large margins built in to protect the contractor in cases of contingency problems. Nevertheless, the guarantee that there would be no cost escalations was perceived by the host as important enough to make the necessary trade-offs. Projects which were completed successfully brought high profits to the supplier, since the share of the total project investment that was under his jurisdiction was higher.

In summary, multinational suppliers are in business to provide quality services and goods to the host customer in a manner that is tailored to the host's particular situation and offers the host a

Figure 3.3

OECD-Six Contractor Portfolios

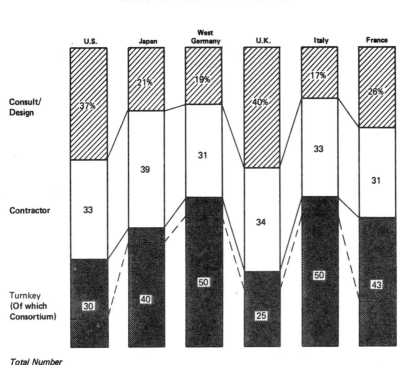

quality or cost advantage over all the other possible supply sources the host might consider evaluating. Multinationals have exhibited a great deal of flexibility, resourcefulness, and expertise in tailoring their services to the needs of the host customers. It would seem advisable to involve them early-on in a project to maximize their understanding of the specifications of the project, and thus enable them to further sharpen the focus and appropriateness of the services they offer, and the bids they make.

4
Approaches to Sponsorship

Every macroproject first originates as a glint in the eye of someone of imagination and vision. Often a single individual evolves a masterplan in his mind about where his country is heading in a developmental sense; how a new technology or massive infrastructural installation can provide a giant step forward for his country; how a new plant can make national entry into global world trade a possibility. Sometimes projects are initiated by a national ministry of industry in the host country, or by a multinational oil or mining company based upon their discovery of a new supply source.

Once the proposed project is regarded as worthy of consideration, a practical, rigorous evaluation process is necessary. A clear project concept must be defined and tested out. Resources must be pulled together. In some cases, the tough decision to delay, put aside, or forget about the project must be made. Diligence is needed in sincerely questioning the project's value in an economic, social, and competitive marketing sense, as well as the local industry's ability to take responsibility for the numerous risks and complex tasks that invariably ensue. Typically, there are long lead times that stand between the first idea and the opening ceremonies of the completed installation.

This chapter describes some of the questions faced by project sponsors in preparing a team to develop and operate a proposed project. Sponsors must push beyond fascination with the possibilities of the project: they must pull together sources of financing, technology, and adequate management capability. Sponsors must prove that they have access to sufficient domestic or international market demand, if the project involves mining or processing a commodity — or that the project will provide adequate social benefits for the costs to be incurred, if the project involves installing infrastructure.

Sponsors must give serious consideration to the long term economic performance of the completed plant — its inherent economic soundness, its international competitiveness. Sponsors need to make thoughtful decisions when structuring the sponsorship arrangement: Projects take a long time to develop, teams will have to last the duration, the stakes are high, and there is a lot to lose if overruns and delays are encountered. Careful evaluation must be made before the sponsorship arrangement is finalized. Specifically, the key players must clearly and carefully:

- Decide their ownership position
- Structure the partnership
- Evaluate the partnership's effectiveness

DECIDING THE OWNERSHIP POSITION

The decision as to whether a sponsor should undertake a project alone or seek outside help appears to be related to the risk factors associated with the project, more than any other variable. When risks are manageable, host sponsors generally maintain 100% equity in the project; when risks are high, joint ventures are the norm.

The internal and external factors associated with high risk projects were described in Chapter 1. Here, it is important to note that certain project industry sectors appear to be more vulnerable to cost escalations and completion delays than others. These can be grouped into three broad categories:

1. High-risk project industries have average cost escalations approaching, and at times exceeding, 100 percent, delays in negotiation, and well over 2 years' delay by the time construction is completed. These include aluminum, copper, power, nickel, petrochemical, and oil/gas projects. Such projects run the greatest risk of being postponed or suspended: Nearly 20 percent of all of these projects have been postponed or suspended (with the exception of power and oil/gas with respective postponement rates of only 6 and 8 percent).

2. <u>Moderate to substantial risk project industries</u> are characterized by average cost escalations of more than 30
percent but less than 100 percent. These include
transportation facilities, steel, other metals, pulp and
paper, chemical minerals, public or social facilities,
fertilizer plants and pipelines. These projects do experience completion delays, but are less likely to be
postponed or suspended. (Only 5 to 6 percent of the
projects per industry segment have been postponed or
suspended.)

3. <u>Low-risk project industries</u> have little if any track record
of cost escalations or completion delays, and are rarely
postponed or suspended once they are undertaken. Such
projects as cement and manufacturing facilities and
communication networks are included here.

Table 4.1 shows how the specific project industries are positioned in
this ranking. It is interesting to note that the magnitude of cost
overruns appears to be increasing rather than decreasing, as the
average cost escalation for projects under construction versus those
completed is well over double the previous percentages, in most
cases.

Project sponsors typically spend a long time studying the
extent of potential risks during the developmental and operational
stages. Their project concept can be described as sound only when
1) the planned project is internally consistent and has adequate
quality checks to ensure that trouble will be identified early and will
be managed in a responsive way; and 2) the project is externally
coherent with the supply/demand and pricing trends in the industry.
The process of fulfilling these two criteria can be a lengthy one.

Multiple feasibility studies are not uncommon, for example:

• On a petrochemical project in Singapore, a Japanese
company conducted four market surveys to determine the
optimal time to gear the project output for entry into the
world market.

• On a petrochemical project in the Philippines, the three
prospective sponsors commissioned four separate feasibility
studies.

• On a steel project in Brazil, three sponsors split feasibility
responsibilities among five committees, each with a representative from the owners.

Table 4.1

Project Industry Risk: Segmentation by Track Record

Risk Level	Average Percent Cost Escalation		Average Number Years Delayed					Postponed/ Suspended		
	Under Construction	Completed	Plan	Negot.	CL	Constr.	Compl.	# of Projects	% of Total	Ave. $MM
High Risk										
Aluminum	267%	110%	6	1	2	3	1	15	18	$ 406
Copper	227	75	–	4	–	5	1	12	18	353
Power	142	40	7	4	–	3	2	13	6	2,014
Nickel	107	45	–	–	–	3	3	6	21	473
Petrochemicals	100	42	–	3	5	3	2	13	12	642
Oil/gas	93	55	–	3	2	2	1	14	8	899
Moderate to Substantial Risk										
Infr: Transport	86%	28%	–	3	1	2	1	10	5	$1,397
Steel	86	50	–	–	–	3	2	6	6	1,727
Other Metals	79	64	–	3	–	3	–	1	3	195

Pulp & Paper	75	8	1	2	1	2	1	1	1	220
Chemical Minerals	45	80	–	2	2	3	3	6	19	165
Infr: Social Facil.	31	0	–	3	–	1	–	6	3	369
Fertilizer	30	20	1	2	2	1	1	5	4	233
Pipelines	–	126	–	3	6	–	1	3	5	983
Low Risk										
(Coal*)	247%	11%	–	2	2	–	–	–	–	$ –
(Mfg: Other*)	253	–	–	–	1	2	2	1	4	170
(Infr: Ind. Facil)	122	–	–	–	–	–	–	–	–	–
Cement	13	–	–	–	3	2	–	–	–	–
Mfg: Electric Eq.	–	–	–	–	–	–	1	–	–	–
Mfg: Transport. Eq	–	–	–	–	–	–	–	–	–	–
Infr: Commun.	–	–	2	–	–	–	–	1	4	15,000
Infr: Govt. Facil.	–	–	–	–	–	–	–	–	–	–

*Very few projects in the sample, but lack of escalation for completed projects, in addition to no postponements, would justify this categorization.

• For the Asahan Aluminum Smelter project in Indonesia, four different countries made feasibility studies — beginning as early as the late 1930s — before the consortium agreement was signed in 1975 (Figure 4.1)

While potential multinational equity partners are most typically involved in the feasibility study, engineering/construction companies and consultants also have participated in these studies.

Figure 4.1

**Chronology of the Asahan Aluminum Smelter Project:
Planning and Negotiation Stages**

The findings of the feasibility study are important in two respects: First, these findings determine the future of the project — whether the proposed project will proceed to the negotiation phase or be postponed, suspended, or abandoned (the fate of one-half of all the jointly owned projects in the planning stage, although some were later revived). Second, the feasibility findings define the relative bargaining position of each prospective participant, setting the stage for the parties' role in the negotiation process.

When to Go It Alone

When the host sponsor has access to enough capital, technology, or global market demand, it can maintain complete ownership of the project, while obtaining the missing items from international suppliers on a contractual basis. The less its financial independence, the more highly competitive the supply/ demand situation, or the more exclusive the required technology, the more inroads guest multinationals can make in obtaining equity ownership or increasing their share of the returns for undertaking a share of project risk.

Host organizations are highly prominent in independently sponsoring macroprojects. A total of 1,067 projects are wholly owned by the hosts.

- Fifty-one percent of the projects involve development of the country's infrastructure. For reasons of national security and sovereignty, a host government never shares ownership of such projects with a foreign company. (There are seven major infrastructure consortia, however, which are multiple-host-government-sponsored projects.)
- The remaining 49 percent are, on the average, small industrial projects, as the country sponsors have allocated only 29 percent of their total investment to these wholly owned projects.

Table 4.2 compares the average size of the industrial projects in the survey. The fact that jointly owned projects are more than twice the size of the host-owned projects suggests that country sponsors extend ownership to guest multinationals when the risks are high and the investments large. It is, of course, quite possible that some of the wholly owned projects that were in the planning stage at the time of this survey have since become joint venture undertakings.

Table 4.2

Ownership Arrangements, Project Size and Stage

Ownership Arrangements	Percentage Of All Projects	Average Size Of Industrial Projects ($ Millions)	Percentage In Planning Stage
Sole host owner(s)	73%	$348	55%
Joint host/guest owners	26	717	17
Sole guest owners	1	490	20

To fully understand the factors that make the host comfortable in sponsoring a project independently, it is helpful to look at the contrasting instances in which they agree to share equity.

When to Joint Venture

In general, as the level of risk increases, so does the likelihood of a decision to form a consortium of companies, composed of international as well as local partners. The purpose is, of course, to insulate any one participant from potentially devastating financial consequences, should the project fail.

The term "consortium" is being consciously substituted for the word joint venture here, as it suggests a more pragmatic basis for collaboration and for negotiating responsibilities and rewards. The parties involved in a consortium join in contracting among themselves to specify the responsibilities of each. Their common features are:

1. They are task-based — Participants are selected on the basis of which project requirements they are capable of satisfying, rather than on who they are or how large an organization they have.

2. They involve risk-sharing — All members assume some measure of risk. Each member's reward is tied to the level of risk assumed, with the payback period being limited to a clearly specified timeframe.

3. There is some competitive advantage — typically, members are selected because of one or more competitive advantage that can be achieved by the unique contributions to be made by a given combination of participants.

The resource consortia referred to here involve joint venture arrangements that are entered into to spread the risks and benefits associated with large-scale resource development projects. At the "macroproject" level of projects, nearly all of these collaborative arrangements are associated with the development and processing of mineral resources.

Observing the project industries in which resource consortia are most prominent, it does appear that resource consortia are very well represented in those project industries that have been designated as "high risk": (Table 4.3)

Table 4.3

Risk Level and Resource Consortia Usage By Project Industry

Project Industry	Risk Level	Number of Consortia	Percent of Total Projects In Segment	Percent Of Total Consortia
Petrochemicals	High	49	43	17
Steel	Moderate	44	42	15
Aluminum	High	41	48	14
Oil refineries	High	26	22	9
Copper	High	23	34	8
Pulp and paper	Moderate	22	31	8
Other metals	High	13	42	4
Fertilizer	Moderate	12	11	4
LNG/LPG	High	12	48	4
Nickel	High	11	38	4

In fact, the decision to form a resource consortium appears to be more related to level of project risk than to the level of development or internal capabilities of the host countries involved, as these collaborative arrangements can be found throughout the developing world in all the project industry sectors under consideration (Figure 4.2), and they are sponsored by some of the most sophisticated of organizations.

Again, collaboration in sponsorship is no reflection on the level of sophistication of the host country, but rather on the daring of the projects being launched, as the countries relying most on this form of cooperation are among the strongest in the developing world — i.e. Saudi Arabia, Brazil, etc., and it is a common form of macroproject development in Australia.

These collaborative undertakings provide an effective way to satisfy important project requirements — their contributions to enhanced effectiveness vary by project industry sector however:

1. For metal mining projects, consortia make it possible to achieve the large capacities necessary to cover infrastructure development costs (sometimes up to 60 percent of total investment) and meet economic criteria. These objectives are more intense of late, as most of the world's

88

Figure 4.2

Resource Consortia by Industry and Location

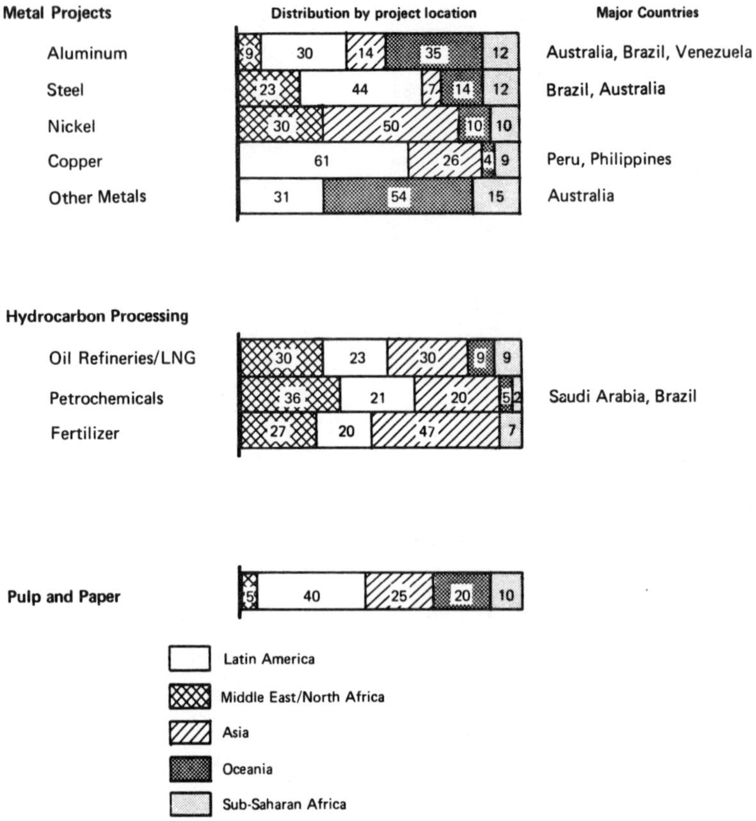

Metal Projects	Distribution by project location	Major Countries
Aluminum	9 / 30 / 14 / 35 / 12	Australia, Brazil, Venezuela
Steel	23 / 44 / 7 / 14 / 12	Brazil, Australia
Nickel	30 / 50 / 10 / 10	
Copper	61 / 26 / 4 / 9	Peru, Philippines
Other Metals	31 / 54 / 15	Australia

Hydrocarbon Processing

Oil Refineries/LNG	30 / 23 / 30 / 9 / 9	
Petrochemicals	36 / 21 / 20 / 5 / 2	Saudi Arabia, Brazil
Fertilizer	27 / 20 / 47 / 7	

Pulp and Paper 5 / 40 / 25 / 20 / 10

- Latin America
- Middle East/North Africa
- Asia
- Oceania
- Sub-Saharan Africa

remaining metal reserves are relatively inaccessible. (The major mining consortia are developing iron, copper, and other metals — 22, 19, and 12, respectively.)

2. For metal and petrochemical processing projects, consortia make it possible for companies to reduce their vulnerabilities to price fluctuations on the output by long-term purchase agreements, and/or allows them to hedge their risks over several projects by lower-risk exposure on each. (The major metal processing consortia are aluminum, and steel facilities — 32 and 22, respectively.)

3. For LNG projects, the need to have a guaranteed buyer and a tailor-made receiving terminal is crucial to justifying the expenditure of constructing such an expensive facility — typically ranging from $500 million to several billion.

4. Oil refineries, by comparison seem to have little problem in finding buyers; thus, the need to form a consortium is greatly diminished.

Overall, the resource consortia provide important vehicles for controlling some of the external risks of a project that are beyond the host's ability to manage alone; and depending upon the strength of the partners, they can also provide technology and managerial assistance that will enhance control of the internal risk factors of these grand-scale projects at the same time.

They attract top companies from the industrialized world. All of the OECD-six countries play some part in macroproject sponsorship via equity-based contracts. Comparing these countries by number of absolute contracts held, Japan heads the list, followed by the United States. The four European countries follow far behind (Table 4.4). The somewhat lower membership of European companies can be attributed to their smaller individual market size, which limits their capacity to make the long-term purchase commitments associated with consortia membership. Relative to market size, however, their participation is substantial.

Table 4.4

**Multinational Resource Consortia Membership
By Country of Origin**

Members From OECD-Six Countries	Number of Companies With Consortia Contracts
Japan	205
United States	139
United Kingdom	37
France	29
Italy	15
West Germany	14

The two most active countries, the United States and Japan, participate in varying degrees in most types of resource development consortia. The United States is better represented than Japan on all but metal processing and pulp and paper projects (Table 4.5).

Table 4.5

U.S. and Japanese Resource Consortia Membership by Project Industry

Project Type	Resource Consortia with Members From			
	United States		Japan	
	Number of Consortia	% of Total Consortia In Sector	Number of Consortia	% of Total Consortia In Sector
Metal processing	26	43%	26	36%
Metal mining	21	35	14	19
Oil Refinery/LNG	13	30	12	27
Petrochemical	19	31	12	20
Pulp and paper	3	15	8	40
Fertilizer	5	33	2	13

The two most typical U.S. members are metal companies and oil companies. The most frequent members from Japan are the trading companies, which are represented on 55 percent of the resource consortia in which Japan participates, and metal companies.

STRUCTURING THE PARTNERSHIP

Once the decision to strike a deal with corporations outside the host country has been made, the complex problem of selecting the right partners and assigning them the appropriate level of exposure and reward surfaces. The job of pulling the partners together is not an easy one. The Redcliff project in Southern Australia illustrates some of the problems that can arise.

- In 1972: Mitsubishi and Alcoa of Australia initiated a petrochemical project to produce caustic soda, polyethylene, and gasoline components from hydrocarbons and salt to be obtained from the Cooper Basin.

- In early 1973: the two companies added two other partners — B. F. Goodrich, which was involved in polyvinyl chloride in Australia, and a group of Japanese trading houses that wanted the liquid petroleum gas for taxis in Tokyo. Then they invited ICI to supplement B. F. Goodrich as another petrochemical end-user.

- In 1974: Objecting to B. F. Goodrich's participation, Dow (which was also competing for development approval) threatened to close its oxichlorination plant in Altoona, Pennsylvania, unless Goodrich withdrew. Next, the Australian government prohibited the export of liquid petroleum gas, so the Japanese trading houses pulled out, leaving only Alcoa, ICI, and Mitsubishi.

- Finally, in 1975, the Australian government insisted on 51 percent Australian ownership in all projects. So the three consortium partners approached three Australian companies. After conducting their own feasibility study, these companies decided that the project was not sufficiently attractive. Then the partners asked five Australian insurance companies to increase their equity. The project was finally abandoned in July 1975.

The problem faced by these prospective collaborators was that they suffered from conflicting purposes and objectives. This long negotiating period could have been shortened if greater clarity of purpose had been sought early-on. On the other hand, changes in governmental policy cannot easily be predicted.

When, as often happens, negotiations drag on longer than expected, they begin to jeopardize the cost and completion estimates worked out in the planning stage, making overruns and delays inevitable. As time passes, costs may escalate and delays lengthen to a point where some prospective sponsors withdraw, unable to participate at the more expensive equity level. And the international market demand and pricing conditions that made the project feasible often will have changed. Moreover, conditions in the host country may have become unfavorable because of changes in the political climate or regulatory environment. Each of these variables can shift the bargaining leverage and alter the would-be sponsors' interest in proceeding with the project.

This section discusses some general notions about how prospective participants decide whether and how to work together. In general, partners should be selected based on what they can contribute to the project, and their contract should be tied to their level of exposure to risks. Contractual supplements to equity offer some alternative possibilities.

Partners Who Can Contribute

Prospective partners offer unique skills and capabilities to a consortium based upon their type of company, country of origin, and any special advantages they have access to because of geographic, financial or other strategic positionings.

Every resource consortium has some representation of resource companies as members (i.e. hydrocarbon processing, metal mining or processing, pulp and paper companies). These companies are principally concerned with benefits they can obtain from the operating facility. Three-quarters of these consortia also have trading companies as members. These companies offer the unique capability of conducting worldwide procurement, managing logistics, and managing the long-term purchase arrangements for the output of the completed plant. Occasionally, equipment manufacturers (who are accessing materials for manufacturing) or government ministries are members (See Figure 4.3).

Figure 4.3

The Resource Consortium: Alternatives for Membership Composition by Type of Organization

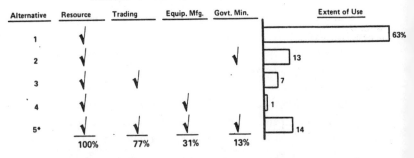

Partners should be selected not only for what they directly bring to the party, but also what they can indirectly offer to meet

Table 4.6

Resource Consortia Member Organizations And Potential Contribution to a Macroproject

Project Requirements	Resource Company	Trading Company	Equipment Manufacturer	Government Ministry
Capital sourcing		Equity capital Loans		Subsidized loans Equity capital Watchdog to ensure that host attains ownership percentage
Technology transfer	Supplier of technology	Procurement logistics	Supplier of capital goods	
Market access	Guaranteed access	Long-term purchase/ trading agreements with sellers and buyers	Guaranteed access (long-term purchase of raw materials for manufacturing)	

94

project requirements across the board — capital sourcing, technology transfer, market access. Additionally, one should examine how the contribution of each will complement that of other prospective members (See Table 4.6).

In addition to the type of organization and business concerns, the question of nationality should be considered. Matches of companies across national borders may provide access to multiple markets or technologies, or competitive financing or other advantages. The most common team in the macroproject survey is a mix between guest nationals from the same industrialized country in partnership with a host organization — more than half of the sample were composed of such a combination (Figure 4.4). Consortia of

Figure 4.4

The Resource Consortium: Alternatives for
Membership Composition by Country of Origin

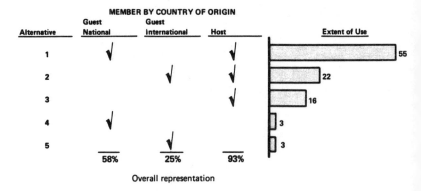

Overall representation

nationals from the same country provide maximum managerial coordination due to shared work styles, customs, and connections; as well as access to government financial backing through such export credit agencies as US and Japan's EXIM, and France's COFACE. International combinations, on the other hand, can syndicate the marketing risks, and provide broad-based technology sources. Nationality has implications for satisfying macroproject requirements, as sketched out in Table 4.7.

Table 4.7

Resource Consortia Member Nationalities and Potential Contributions to a Macroproject

Project Requirements	Guest Nationals	Guest Nationals and Host	Guest Internationals and Host	Host
Capital sourcing	Private sourcing from guest country	Government backing from host (special incentives) or guest (special financing)	Private sourcing	Government backing from host
Technology transfer	Maximum coordination	Host assistance in integrating with local environment	Broad-based sourcing of technology, with local coordination	Use of local E/C or locally produced capital goods
Market access	Home country or local access to market	Preferential access to market	Syndicated market risk over multiple country markets	Local markets

Table 4.8

Competitors As Resource Consortia Members: Complementary Responsibilities

Trombetus River Bauxite Consortium

Owners of the Resource 51% Equity	End Users of the Resource 49% Equity			
Host Sponsor	Competitive Member Companies	Country	Equity %	Output %
Cia. Vale do Rio Doce Brazil 37% Output	Alcan Aluminum (sponsor)	Canada	19	22
	Shell	Netherlands	5	
	Norsk Hydro	Norway	5	14
	AS Ardal og Sunndalverk	Norway	5	
	Instituto Nacional de Industria	Spain	5	7
	Rio Tinto Zinc Corporation	United Kingdom	5	7
	Reynolds Aluminum do Brasil	United States	5	7
	Rio Xingir	Netherlands		

Equity Based on Exposure

Once the partners are selected, the challenge begins. The optimum mix of skills and resources needs to be determined. There are numerous fascinating examples of how competitors in the international arena have been brought into harmony of purpose and commonality of goals on these macroprojects.

The Trombetus River Bauxite Consortium in Brazil, for one, is the result of the teaming up of a group of competitors — all motivated by the need for a raw material source that each member lacked but that no single member could have developed alone because of the risks involved. On that project, the owner of the resource — Cia Vale do Rio Doce (Brazil) — and a consortium of guest multinationals with market access privileges undertook equity in a joint venture company, Mineracao Rio do Norte, S.A. (Table 4.8). Since the consortium intended to make Brazil one of the world's largest bauxite producers, such a mix of users and access to such a range of markets were critical to justifying the go-ahead for such an endeavor. For the end-users, access to a secured supply of raw materials, available by consortium participation, is a means of diversifying sources of supply over multiple projects. Each such project has an effect on the world market similar to that of a cartel.

Some combinations of unlikely partners in complementary business activities can also make sense — that is, when their combined strengths satisfy the complete mix of project requirements. The Bintulu Liquified Natural Gas project in Sarawak, Malaysia, is a good example of this type of team formation. Petronas, the national oil company, held 65 percent equity and owned the gas to be liquified. Shell and Mitsubishi shared the remaining equity at 17.5 percent each. Shell discovered the gas and supplied it to the project under a production-sharing contract. Shell also designed the plant and supervised construction and start-up. Mitsubishi agreed to buy 100 percent of the output for a 20 year period (Table 4.9). Clearly, the arrangement is complementary, based on compatible expertise: Shell's main tasks in the project are technological, Mitsubishi's are market-related, and Petronas is the owner and provider of the resource.

Among the many equity arrangements, some of the most interesting are the resource consortia organized by Japan and a host

Table 4.9

**Non-Competitors As Resource Consortia Members:
Complementary Responsibilities**

Bintulu LNG Project, Sarawak, Malaysia		
Majority Owner Of the Resource	Developer/ Project Manager	Marketer of Output
Petronas (65% equity)	Shell (17% equity)	Mitsubishi (17.5% equity)
	- Supply gas under production-sharing contract	- Market LNG in Japan (20-year contract)
	- Design the plant and supervise construction and start-up as technical consultant	

country. These consortia are "national projects," of strategic importance to Japan. Since Japan is dependent on imports for ninety percent of its raw materials, its national ministry of industry, MITI, plays an active role in marshalling projects and domestic industry support to maintain a steady raw material supply. Participation in the development phase is not their main objective, although they typically monitor their projects thoroughly in that phase. The Japanese government's interest in forming these national consortia is to purchase the output on a long-term basis.

For each so-called national project, the Japanese form a separate company consisting of representatives from all of the relevant industry sectors, as well as a syndicate of commercial banks (usually including the banks associated with the trading companies). Equity participation of all Japanese companies in an industry sector on one of these projects has the effect of equalizing raw material risks and costs for competitors after the same source. Frequent government participants are the Overseas Economic Cooperation Fund (OECF) and the Japan Export-Import Bank (EXIM Bank). From such backers, members of the national consortium sometimes receive up to 80 percent of the financing required in debt at low interest rates (Table 4.10). Upon formation, the national

Table 4.10

Japanese National Project Consortium Company:
Typical Format

Capital Structure	Typical Consortium Composition
Equity ($\pm$20%)	Mining (or other) companies Manufacturing companies Trading companies Syndicate of commercials banks
Debt ($\pm$80%)	OECF EXIM Bank Japanese Int'l. Cooperation Agency

project consortium company then enters a two-party joint venture with the host participant, taking equity in the company. An example of such an arrangement is the Alumina do Brasil project (Table 4.11).

Table 4.11

Example of Japanese National Project Consortia:
Alumina do Brasil Project

Alumina do Brasil (ALBRAS) 100%

(Joint Venture Company)

Cia Vale do Rio Doce, Brazil, 51%	Light Metal Smelter 49% (Japanese Consortium)	
	Japanese Consortium Members	
	Private 60%	Public 40%
	• 5 Smelters	54% EXIM Bank
	• 6 Aluminum rolling mills	32% Major Japan Banking Group
	• 8 Consumers	12% OECF
	• 9 Trading Companies	2% Japanese corporations

Usually, a single company will represent the consortium as lead participant. These projects may be proposed to the host country by MITI or the lead company. It also occurs that host governments approach MITI with a proposal. The fact that these consortia are completely packaged to include financing and long term purchase increases Japan's bargaining leverage with the host sponsors.

While this Japanese format has been applied on several projects, no consortium format should be selected without careful consideration of its suitability for the particular project in question. Each equity decision should be based on what is the very best arrangement for the project, not on what arrangement worked before, or for someone else. The Japanese have been quite creative in adapting their contractual exposure to what they are able to give to a project, and what they hope to get in return for their participation (Figure 4.5). They are willing to take lower equity positions when they have less at stake.

Figure 4.5

Japanese Partnership Packages

| FORMAT | JAPANESE CONTRIBUTION | | | EXAMPLE | ADVANTAGE TO JAPAN |
	Capital	Technology	Market		
90 Percent Japanese Equity	X	X	X	Asahan (30-year)	Maintains confidentiality of technology
50 Percent Japanese Equity: Mine; Smelter; Trading Companies; Banks; Government	X	±	X	Belem Aluminum Brazil	Ensures • Low-cost debt • Competitive fairness on home market • Long-term purchase of output
3-Way Venture: U.S. Metal Company and Japanese Trading Company and Host			X	Australian Metal Projects	Fills Japan's raw material needs without requiring technology transfer
Less Than 10 Percent Japanese Equity Plus Long-Term Purchase Contract	±		X	Robe River; Nippon Steel 30 Percent Equity for 40 Percent Output Of Iron Ore	Can diversify raw material supply via low equity on many projects, thereby hedging on risk Participates in decision making, thus gaining access to price-setting system
No Japanese Equity; Loan and Long-Term Purchase Contract	X		X	Badak and Arun LNG	Assures fixed quantity of mineral supply in repayment of loan

The Japanese are far more flexible than U.S. companies in varying their equity posture (Figure 4.6). The U.S. equity share per participant in the consortia to which they belong is generally higher than for the average Japanese participant. The U.S. members can be found to hold at least 21 percent equity or more on over 50 percent of the consortia in which they participate in the metal

Figure 4.6

Profile of U.S. and Japanese
Equity Share in Resource Consortia

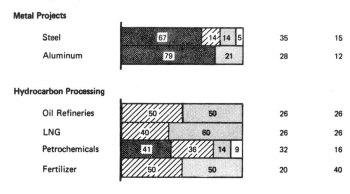

A. Patterns of U.S. participation

Metal Projects	Distribution of Participants by percent equity held	Average percent equity Per Project	Per Participant
Steel	43 / 43 / 14	34	29
Aluminum	40 / 40 / 13	34	24

Hydrocarbon Processing

Oil Refineries	66 / 37	50	33
LNG	33 / 50 / 22	14	11
Petrochemicals	50 / 50	50	50
Fertilizer	75 / 25	33	33

B. Patterns of Japanese participation

Metal Projects

Steel	67 / 14 / 14 / 5	35	15
Aluminum	79 / 21	28	12

Hydrocarbon Processing

Oil Refineries	50 / 50	26	26
LNG	40 / 60	26	26
Petrochemicals	41 / 36 / 14 / 9	32	16
Fertilizer	50 / 50	20	40

Percent equity held

 < 10%   11 – 20   21 – 49   □ 50 +

industries, whereas Japanese companies typically hold less than a 10 percent share. It is not uncommon to find a large number of Japanese companies — particularly trading companies — syndicating the high risks associated with mineral development projects. In hydrocarbon processing the variation in modes of involvement is more accentuated, as the U.S. members can be found to pass the 50 percent equity mark in a quarter to a half of the cases (except LNG), whereas the Japanese rarely do.

Contractual Supplements

It should be noted that, while high risk provides a strong motive to share equity, there are strong pressures within most host countries to keep foreign equity to a minimum. The first sign of the host's strong position in this regard was the rash of oil company nationalizations after the 1973 crisis. Even non-OPEC regional organizations in the developing world have adopted regulations designed to limit foreign equity or provide for reversion of ownership after a specified period — one such case is the Andean Pact nations. Such regulations, some observers believe, are by no means wholly bad news for the foreign investor, since countries that impose them may be likely to honor contractual commitments more faithfully in the interim.

Thus, where formerly a participant could count on negotiating an equity arrangement that reflected its contribution to the project, more and more, host governments are regulating the share of allowable foreign ownership and using other means to bind participants to the partnership. The real-life implications of these changes in the ground rules can be seen in the equity posture which host organizations are maintaining on the various resource consortia currently active in the developing countries. Figure 4.7 shows that host sovereignty is strictly preserved in the hydrocarbon processing industries, but is currently less evident among metal mining and processing projects. In such project industries where host sovereignty is preserved, the 50/50 split in equity is more common than might be expected. Petrochemical projects are equal partnerships in over half the cases.

Equity is not necessarily the only bargaining tool available to the host in attempting to diminish and/or share risks. With the rise in limitations on foreign ownership and the concomitant erosion of

Figure 4.7

Profile of Host Equity Posture in Resource Consortia

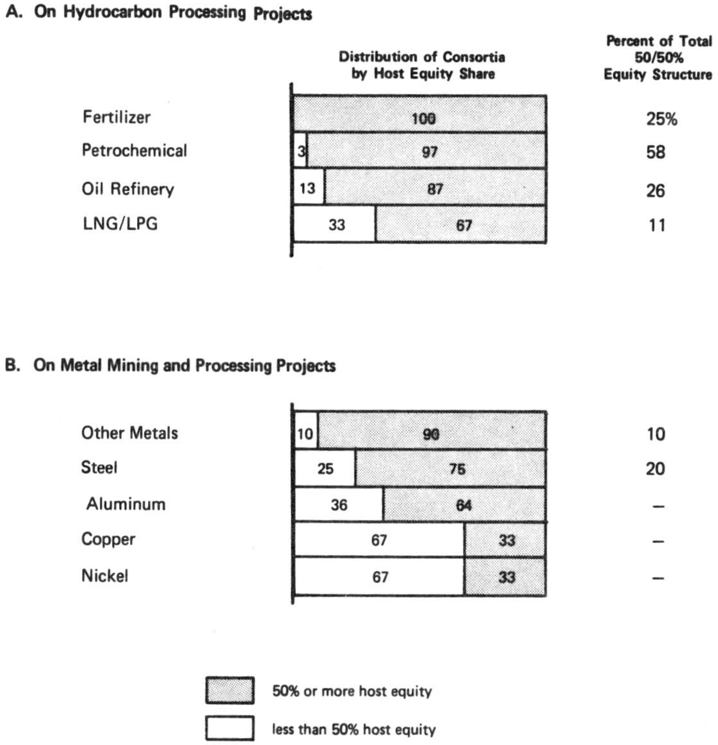

A. On Hydrocarbon Processing Projects

	Distribution of Consortia by Host Equity Share	Percent of Total 50/50% Equity Structure
Fertilizer	100	25%
Petrochemical	3 | 97	58
Oil Refinery	13 | 87	26
LNG/LPG	33 | 67	11

B. On Metal Mining and Processing Projects

Other Metals	10 | 90	10
Steel	25 | 75	20
Aluminum	36 | 64	—
Copper	67 | 33	—
Nickel	67 | 33	—

▨ 50% or more host equity

☐ less than 50% host equity

equity rights, a variety of contractual mechanisms have been
devised to enable participants to continue to make their contributions to the project, and to reap their profits from it. Table 4.12
shows some of the contractual supplements that consortia members
are using to share risk, and the advantages and disadvantages of
each. (In cases where equity is not desirable, these supplements
can, in fact, become substitutes for equity.) These include
production sharing contracts, concessionary financing, suppliers'
credits, long-term purchase contracts, coproduction agreements (or
barter or payment in kind), and loan and repayment in output.

On the Badak and Arun LNG projects in Indonesia, Pertamina,
the national oil company, was extremely resourceful in making use
of these contractual alternatives to avoid diluting equity. On both

Table 4.12

Contractual Supplements to Equity: Examples

Contractual Supplement	Risks Shared	Advantages
Production sharing	Exploration and development costs	Nonowners are normally paid a fee or an agreed percent after cost recovery in exchange for assuming the exploration risks and development costs
Concessionary financing	Infrastructure costs	Low-interest, long-term financing diminishes economic impact of costs
Suppliers' credits	Capital goods transfer and delivery risks	Financing from supplier provides more flexibility and guarantees to purchaser
Long-term purchase contract	Market inaccessibility	Buyers agree to provide a distribution system for output in exchange for a guarantee of supply
Coproduction (or barter or payment in kind)	Technological and market inaccessibility	Output replaces capital
Buyers' Consortium	Economies of scale	A consortium of buyers can permit increased capacity utilization on a guaranteed basis
Loan and repayment in output	Capital return	Output replaces capital

of these projects Pertamina maintained 100 percent equity ownership of the plant and equipment by establishing a package of
supplementary contracts. The Badak structure illustrates this
(Table 4.13). Huffco, a consortium of small oil companies from the

Table 4.13

Contractual Supplements to Equity:
Badak LNG Project, Indonesia

Contract	Organization(s) involved
Production sharing	Huffco Consortium, U.S.
Loan and repayment in kind	Bank of Tokyo Industrial Bank of Japan
Buyers' credits	EXIM Japan
Project management	Bechtel, U.S.
Long-term purchase	Chuba Electric, Japan

U.S., had a production-sharing contract to supply the gas; the
Japanese supplied financing under buyers' credit and loan and
repayment in kind agreements. Bechtel, U.S., provided project
management expertise. Chuba Electric of Japan will receive 100
percent of the output under a long-term purchase contract.

While Pertamina has complete sovereignty over the plant and
facility they have not maintained complete control over the
operating organization: They hold only a 55 percent share of the
operating company, P.T. Badak Natural Gas Liquification Company.
The Japanese consortium of buyers, led by Chuba, and the Huffco
group, each has an equity share in the operating company (15 and 30
percent respectively).

The real catch to achieving a mutually satisfying and enduring
partnership is to strike a fair balance between the risks to be
assumed and the reward to be gained by each participant. It is
often the case, however, that the power relationship among hosts
and multinational guests can change during the long project
lifecycle. Thus it is not always possible to define a firm
risk/reward structure at the outset. In most cases, the leverage of
the foreign companies is probably at its peak as the project begins,

Table 4.14

Contractual Approaches to Contingency Protection

Project Requirement	Contingency	Contractual Protection
Capital sourcing	Host changes regulations governing - Local taxes - Recomputations - Expropriations	- Renegotiation clause with prior agreement on schedule - Phaseout or limited life - Quick payback via lowered taxes, thus reducing foreign risk
Technology transfer	Inflation and interest rates affect construction costs	- Escalator clauses - Contingency clauses - Quotations made in guest country currency - Inflation rate built into bid
Market access	Commodity prices fluctuate sharply	Long-term purchase - Fixed base price and cost increases and escalations (maximum = only 50 percent of the difference in increase between fixed and market price) - Actual cost and profit agreed in advance (0 to 6 years–0%, 7 to 12 years–6%, 13 to 18 years–10%)

and the host's need of technological, or financial assistance is most acute. As the risks are overcome and the project nears completion, the leverage of the host improves significantly. Accordingly, participants have found that the duration of particular commitments needs to be spelled out with great care. Innovative contractual agreements have been found to address some of the critical problems. Some contractual devices to protect participants against the contingencies that could adversely affect their profitability are sketched out in Table 4.14. These include expropriations, changes in local taxes, interest or inflation rates, or commodity price fluctuations.

Besides concern for the equity structure of a project, it is also important to work out how the operating company will be organized and operated.

Long-term purchase arrangements, whether or not tied to equity, do have implications for the way in which the operating company is to be structured. It is important that these operational considerations be resolved early on, as they can have an important impact on the design and construction requirements of the facility. Metal projects in particular need careful forward planning with respect to distribution of the output, as it can effect the construction parameters of the contract. Similarly, LNG purchase contracts usually demand that a loading port be constructed at the receiving end. Some interesting marketing arrangements are being written into the partnership agreements of the consortia members to satisfy the interests of all. To highlight three:

1. Partners in an iron ore mine in Australia established an equitable system for distributing the resource by establishing a separate production company (Figure 4.8A):

    • The joint venture partners established a production organization whose responsibility it is to produce the ore and deliver it to the partners who will then sell it. This organization is not profit-making but produces a fixed tonnage per year based on preset tonnage and quality orders agreed upon by the partners.
    • Each partner pays a management fee to the production company.

- All distribution is based on an ore year, and a yearly production, sales and shared distribution scheme is drawn each year; its share for the next year will be raised to compensate for amounts not taken in the previous year.
- Partners can sell ore for varying prices; only quantity is assured.
- Should a more expensive ore (i.e., silver) be mined, the quantity would be divided into equal shares among the partners.

Figure 4.8

Implications of Long-Term Purchase Arrangements On the Operating Company Structure

A. An iron ore mine, Australia

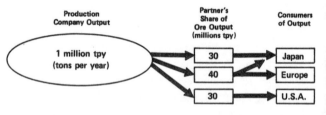

B. An iron ore mine, Brazil

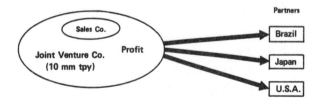

C. A steel plant, Brazil

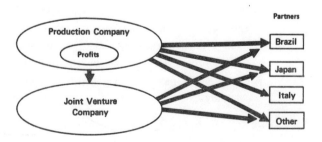

2. <u>Partners in an iron ore mine in Brazil</u> preserved the local ownership of the joint venture company while assuring a payback for foreign investors by establishing rights to dividends (Figure 4.8B):

    • Partners put up money but have no share of output. All shares are transferred through the sales company which is part of the joint venture company. Since Brazil prohibits foreign ownership of joint venture companies, the entity is regarded as a Brazilian company.

    • After calculating the mining and administrative costs, the sales price is set and the resulting profit is apportioned among the partners who are guaranteed a dividend for participation. The net profit, after retained earnings, is distributed according to percent equity.

    • However, these are separate purchase contracts between the joint venture company and each of the partners as customers, regarding the purchase of output.

3. <u>Partners in a steel plant in Brazil</u> established fairness by allowing rights to output equal to equity but assured quality standards by allowing sales to other parties and rights to dividends (Figure 4.8C):

    • Three companies are entitled to a tonnage of the plant output equal to their percent equity ownership.

    • The companies place their orders twice a year, announcing each month's schedule, volume, and quality for each of the six months. Any production error that does not meet the quality standards is sold as a byproduct or scrap. The profit from such a sale would go to the joint venture company and be distributed at the end of the year.

    • To assure fairness in distribution, the joint venture company has a board of directors and supervisors composed of representatives of each of the partners' companies. In addition, the three partners are represented by all important personnel in production and distribution.

In summary, every decision to form a partnership has managerial, organizational — and even structural — implications for the project.

EVALUATING THE PARTNERSHIP'S EFFECTIVENESS

The most appropriate partners may have been selected for a given project, however further evaluation must be made to determine how the members will interface organizationally to achieve long-term effectiveness. Based on the survey of macroprojects in the 1970s, it has been found that the structure and composition of resource consortia membership appears to influence the overall effectiveness of the partnership.

While the principal purpose of entering a resource consortium is to share the risks as well as the benefits of resource development, membership does not, in itself, guarantee safety. Striking the right balance between equity and contractual commitments; between local and foreign companies in the partnership; between syndicating and assuming responsibility can impact the final outcome of the project. The effectiveness of any particular structure appears to vary by project industry.

Predominance of the Host

It appears that the extent of problems encountered on projects with majority host equity is usually lower than that on projects where the host is in a minority equity position. This suggests that a dominant posture by the host might serve the positive function of marshalling local support for a project and in stabilizing the local environment in which the project is being developed. The fact that host sponsors are still able to marshall the necessary support to undertake these macroprojects also suggests that the consortia probably include some market access and technological support obtained on a contractual basis or that the output is destined for the domestic market. This trend appears to be consistent by project industry sector (Figure 4.9).

Since most hydrocarbon processing projects have more than 50 percent host equity, it is important to distinguish the 50/50 equity split from other arrangements (Table 4.15): In general, the higher the host equity, the better the track record of the projects — with the exception of oil refineries and LNG for which the 50/50 structure works slightly more efficiently with respect to minimizing overruns, although delays are, on average, higher.

When the averages for incidence of difficulties faced by the hydrocarbon processing project consortia are compared with those

Figure 4.9

Track Record of Resource Consortia
By Host Equity Posture

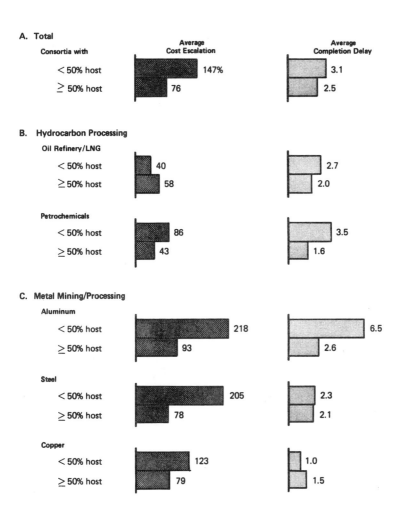

encountered by metal project consortia, one can observe the more
severe troubles faced by metal developers. However, when this
overall track record is compared with the totals for all projects, it
is apparent that consortia are slightly more effective at containing
cost and time overruns than sole host owners for this type of
project. As already noted in Table 4.1, oil and gas projects have a

55 to 93 percent record of overruns and 1- to 3-year delays for the total sample of projects. This compares with 40 to 58 percent escalations and roughly 2-year delays for the resource consortia. Similarly, for all petrochemical projects, the overall track record of 42 to 100 percent escalations and 2- to 5-year delays as compared

Table 4.15

Host Equity Share and Magnitude of Trouble: Selected Project Industries

Host Equity Share:	50%		More than 50%	
Average:	CE(%)	CD (yrs)	CE(%)	CD(yrs)
Project Industry				
Petrochemical	86%	3.5 yrs	43%	1.6 yrs
Oil refinery/LNG	40	2.7	58	2.0

with resource consortia that have, on average, 43 to 86 percent overruns and 1.6- to 3.5-year delays. Thus, while majority host equity is beneficial, total host equity may not always be advisable.

Internationality

The more international the combination of members, the more troublesome the track records for such projects. In fact, the more complex the mix of members, the more vulnerable the project (Table 4.16). Noting the percent of resource consortia projects that

Table 4.16

Resource Consortia Membership Mix and Trouble Rate

Resource Consortium Mix	Trouble Rate
Guest nationals only	9%
Guest nationals and host	42
International guests	60
International guests and host	70
Multiple Hosts	44

experienced some type of cost escalation or completion delay, the incidence of trouble is significantly higher for consortia that include a mix of multinational guests of differing nationalities — with or without a host partner — as compared with consortia with multinationals from the same country of origin. Frequently, the guest national is a single company, as will be discussed in the next section.

Without further indepth analysis, one must use these findings with caution, as there are so many competitive advantages to assembling such teams. The higher incidence of trouble could be related to the fact that the projects might be more complex — therefore the need, in the first place, to attract such broad-based support. More importantly, this suggests that whatever the attraction in building such partnerships, prospective members should be cautioned to be particularly diligent in setting up a clear decision-making procedure. They must ensure that the conflicts in values and workstyles that are likely to arise will be counter-balanced by clear groundrules for day-to-day decision-making, and a common vision and set of goals.

When we look at the magnitude of difficulties, rather than merely the frequency with which they have been found to encounter

Figure 4.10

**Track Record of Resource Consortia
By Extent of Internationality**

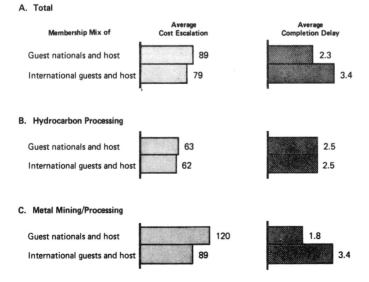

trouble, it appears that the more international teams experience more completion delays than less diverse teams; however, their average cost escalations are not significantly higher (Figure 4.10).

Extent of Syndication

A survey of macroprojects shows that the more syndicated the risks — and therefore the more numerous the membership and the less vulnerable each individual member — the more likely the project will be to experience cost escalations, completion delays, or other setbacks.

Multipartite consortia are, on the average, twice as likely to run into trouble as two-party arrangements (Table 4.17). This

Table 4.17

Resource Consortia Membership Syndication and Incidence of Trouble

Consortia Membership	Number	Percent	Trouble Rate
Two-party	95	50%	25%
Multipartite	96	50	44
	191	100%	

suggests that the more complex decision-making process that results from numerous members of a partnership may be a factor in complicating the efficiency of these projects. (Again, the projects, in themselves, might be more complex.) Nevertheless, diminishing risks by expanding membership can, in itself, present additional risks, unless clear responsibilities and tasks are defined. There are different ways that multiple partners can create more problems than they solve: 1) they might require monitoring of the project by committee, which encumbers decision-making and can create unclear lines of authority between the owners, the project managers, and those the project manager supervises; or 2) they may be too distant from the project, on the other hand, and refuse to support, or be unable to support, the project in times of difficulty or crisis, whether due to political, financial or logistical disruption.

However, the extent of trouble encountered does not, on average, vary significantly for two-party versus multipartite con-

Figure 4.11

Track Record of Resource Consortia
By Level of Syndication

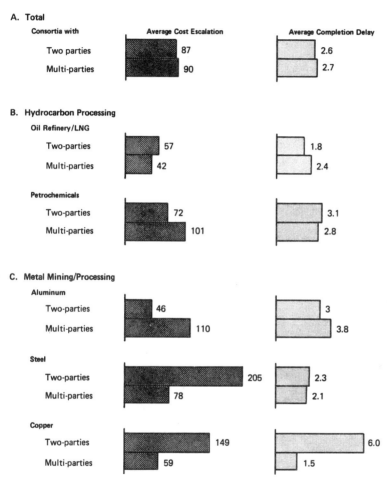

A. Total

| Consortia with | Average Cost Escalation | Average Completion Delay |

Two parties — 87 — 2.6
Multi-parties — 90 — 2.7

B. Hydrocarbon Processing

Oil Refinery/LNG
Two-parties — 57 — 1.8
Multi-parties — 42 — 2.4

Petrochemicals
Two-parties — 72 — 3.1
Multi-parties — 101 — 2.8

C. Metal Mining/Processing

Aluminum
Two-parties — 46 — 3
Multi-parties — 110 — 3.8

Steel
Two-parties — 205 — 2.3
Multi-parties — 78 — 2.1

Copper
Two-parties — 149 — 6.0
Multi-parties — 59 — 1.5

sortia.   On a project industry basis, some differences do emerge. On a cost control basis, the multipartite ventures are more efficient for oil refineries, LNG, iron and copper mines, and steel mills.   On a schedule basis, they are only significantly more effective on copper projects (Figure 4.11).   This again suggests that the need for day-to-day coordination among multiple participants is critical when the numerous members play a part in the day-to-day coordination and monitoring of the project.   However, as discussed earlier, many of these multipartite consortia are providing marketing as well as other support for projects whose output is destined for export. Delays can be deliberately planned to achieve better economics after start-up. As discussed earlier, projects are best scheduled to come on stream at a point when market demand can comfortably be forecast as favorable and thus the prices the joint venture partners can set for the output can be economically attractive. Correct timing can significantly enhance returns to the shareholders.

It is interesting to note that of those projects which have not experienced any trouble to date, 63 percent are two-party consortia (this is 67 percent for metals and 59 percent for hydrocarbon processing).

As discussed earlier, the Japanese are the most noted participants for the extent to which they rely on syndication as a vehicle for investing in macroprojects. Often their national project

Figure 4.12

**Track Record of Macroprojects Sponsored
By Japanese National Consortia and Host Partners**

PROJECT	Original ($MM)	Current ($MM)	Escalation (Percent)	Original	Current	Delay (Years)
Belem Aluminum Complex (Brazil)	$2,500	$5,000	100%	1973	1977	4
Guyana Aluminum Smelter (Venezuela)	212	550	159	1978	1980	2
Asahan Aluminum Smelter (Indonesia)	870	2,000	130	1983	1984/83	0-1
Michiguillay Copper Mine (Peru)	280	800	186	1982	Postponed	
Wologesi Iron Mine (Liberia)	600	1,000	67	1980	Abandoned/ Feasibility revived	
Camacari Petrochemical Complex (Brazil)	1,200	3,000	150	1977	1980	
Merbau Island Petrochemical Complex (Singapore)	700	2,000 to 926 (Scaled Down)	186 to 32	1977	1982	5
Bandar Shahpur Petrochemical Complex (Iran)	1,000	3,300	230	1982	1984	2
Al Jubail Petrochemical Complex (Saudi Arabia)	1,000	2,000 to 1,800 (Scaled Down)	100 to 80	1981	1985	4
Minas Gerais Pulp Mill (Brazil)	220	240	9	1976	1977	1

PROJECTED COST — COMPLETION SCHEDULE

consortia include up to 36 different companies as partners. While they do represent a brilliant effort at pooling large sums of capital and resources, and while they are extremely creative in neutralizing any competitive advantages among companies in the home industry, they are also highly vulnerable — as can be seen by the track record to date of these national project consortia throughout the 1970s (Figure 4.12). The total unexpected cost escalation for these important projects adds up to more than $11 billion. While the list includes some of the more preemptive projects around, the Japanese have been far more creative in formulating innovative financing and marketing solutions than in ushering these projects swiftly through their feasibility and developmental phases. Again the project concepts are so highly complex that delays could indeed represent the very best strategy they could have undertaken. Nevertheless, the unexpected cost and time commitments cannot but be perceived by the managers in the home offices in Tokyo as unwelcome and to be avoided in the future.

Although it is not possible to evaluate the individual impact of U.S. and Japanese members on more diverse consortia, it is possible to look at their overall experiences in the macroproject arena by

Figure 4.13

Track Record of Resource Consortia with U.S. and Japanese Members

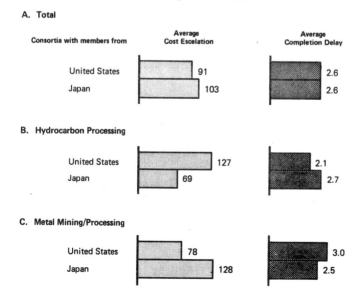

summarizing the track records of the consortia to which they belonged. On an aggregate basis, projects with Japanese members were slightly more prone to cost overruns, but the delay rate was the same as that for U.S.-member consortia (Figure 4.13). However, there are clear differences by industry: The projects with U.S. members experienced more serious overruns on hydrocarbon processing projects, and longer delays on the metal projects. Projects with Japanese partners showed the inverse trend: Their metal projects overran more and their hydrocarbon processing projects had longer delays.

Some guidelines for setting up an effective basis for collaboration are described in Chapters 6 and 7. Sponsors do not have to develop the projects alone. They can contract out parts of the project to engineering/construction and other firms. The ways guest multinationals cooperate in the transfer of technology are described in the following chapter.

5
Cooperation in Technology Transfer

The resource consortium model discussed in the previous chapter is composed of members whose primary interest is in the functioning of the operational facility. They look at the development phase as a means to an end. There is an entire other group of players whose primary interest is in providing engineering services and process technologies to the project as it is being developed. Depending upon whether the sponsors are in possession of the process technology or have in-house engineering capability, or need to access technology from international sources on a contractual basis, the opportunities for these independent technology providers can vary. In general, they can provide design, engineering, construction, or equipment 1) on a partial basis; 2) in a package — either on an independent turnkey contract or as member of a contractors' consortium; or 3) they might coordinate the entire development for the owner under a project management contract.

The fact that host organizations can purchase an entire plant or infrastructure facility on a packaged or turnkey basis considerably extends their range of options for implementing their national development plans. Host sponsors who do not wish to relinquish control in exchange for needed technology or managerial expertise may choose to delegate control of the development of their project to international contractors. They are able to carefully select among companies with considerable experience in transferring the relevant technology, and in minimizing or making the most of the unexpected problems and risks that inevitably emerge. The turnkey approach is most commonly used on macroprojects for which market access or the confidentiality or need for carefully tailored technology are not at issue. For example:

- On infrastructure projects such as power, transport, universities, new towns, sewage systems, and the like.
- On industrial development projects where the output is destined for the local market (e.g., a pulp and paper factory constructed in Iraq), where market access is already established (e.g., expansion of an oil refinery in Iran), and particularly on processing projects where technologies are sold by chemical or metallurgical engineering firms.

While many contractors offer to assume turnkey responsibility on an individual basis and then subcontract out parts of the job once the contract is won, there is also a growing number of contractors who at the outset are offering to undertake these obligations in collaboration with others. This chapter focuses on the role that international engineering and construction firms — among others — play in transferring technology to macroprojects in the developing world. In particular, the contractors' consortium will be evaluated against other alternatives to assess the advantages, workings, and problems of these efforts in transnational cooperation.

Contractors interested in participating in the macroproject arena need to determine what the host sponsors require of them, and what they can most competitively contribute. Sound cooperation is achieved when contractors:

- Identify the technological gaps
- Competitively provide the missing technology
- Ensure synergy in delivery of the technology
- Anticipate potential problem areas.

IDENTIFYING THE TECHNOLOGICAL GAPS

The technologies being transferred from the OECD nations to the developing world are broadly defined here to include the managerial, engineering, design, and process technologies necessary to conceptualize, design, engineer, construct and start up a macroproject facility. There are gaps that remain after local organizations and joint venture partners have made their respective contributions. Some of the technological gaps exist because process technologies are in the complete possession of OECD multinationals and can only be obtained from them. Other gaps exist because of project management and control deficiencies in the host country — due either to overall scarcity of management talent or to the complexity of the individual project itself.

Each developing country has its own portfolio of skills and capabilities that it can readily commit to a macroproject. The best international competitors are those who are able to incorporate these host strengths into their overall bid package, while at the same time providing the multinational skills which the host is sorely in need of. This requires assessment. Briefly, the two generic types of gaps that can be found are:

1. Process Technology Gaps. Sponsors let contracts to international suppliers most frequently in industries with the most restrictive regulation of majority foreign equity (e.g., hydrocarbon processing) and/or in industries where the processing technologies are constantly changing — requiring continual evaluation, selection and modification. The essential technologies are frequently in the hands of those who are not interested in making a risk-bearing equity commitment to the project. Therefore, they can only be accessed on a contractual basis through the engineering or construction company or equipment manufacturer who holds the license or owns the technology.

2. Project Management Gaps. When host sovereignty or host equity is not at issue — in civil works such as transportation and power facilities, and in major public works such as new cities, towns, housing — host sponsors may find it difficult to provide the highly sophisticated management coordination necessary to complete these highly visible projects on time and within budget. The host frequently turns to international firms to assume this managerial task. This essentially involves ensuring synergy in coordinating the various components of these elaborate projects.

The gaps that have been filled over the 1970s can be seen by the extent and type of contracts won by international firms. Figure 5.1 shows the number and types of contracts won by international engineering/construction companies by project industry type. The bulk of the consulting and design contracts are in the hydrocarbon processing industries, followed by infrastructure development efforts

122

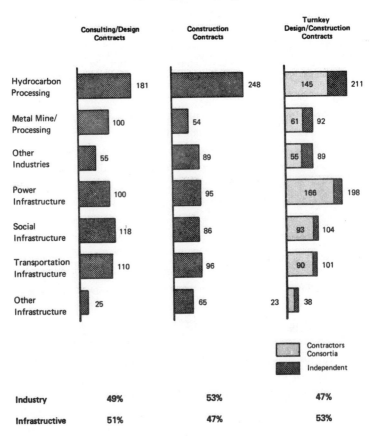

Figure 5.1

**Profile of Contracts Awarded
By Project Industry**

in the social, transport and power areas.   There are numerous independent construction contracts for all types of macroprojects, the largest number again in the hydrocarbon processing area. Turnkey contracts which include design, procurement, project management, and start-up responsibilities can be awarded either to consortia or to single companies who then subcontract out pieces of the work. The consortium approach is typically on a fixed fee basis, whereas the independent turnkey or design/construct contract may be cost-plus, depending upon how well conceptualized the project is and how well the subcontractor costs have been worked out, among other concerns. In the macroproject arena, consortia are used for projects where process technologies can be installed efficiently on a "plant-export" basis — that is, in a total package with minimal infrastructural complications. Turnkey contracts are important modes for supplying technology in hydrocarbon processing and power — in particular, oil refineries, fertilizer and ethylene plants, coal-, oil-fired, and nuclear power — projects with few, if any, geotechnical issues to confront. On hydroelectric projects, design and construction of the dam and water tunnel can be complex. Consortia of designers are more and more frequently found on these projects, sharing the risks in designing these multi-billion dollar projects. Often, consortia of contractors follow, supplying the equipment, process, and engineering and construction capability.

Not all guest multinationals are facing the same degree of competition in providing capital goods and engineering services to these macroprojects. In fact, there are groups of companies who currently stand unparalleled either in the services they are providing, or in their flexibility with regard to the types of contracts they are willing to assume. Others find themselves facing intense competition in trying to win one of these contracts.

The real distinctions in technology transfer are between separate design and consultancy contracts which are then passed on to contractors, and the turnkey approach which includes design. It appears that firms in the United States are particularly dominant in providing design, consulting, and project management services, while those in France, Italy, West Germany, and the United Kingdom dominate in turnkey arrangements, although their consulting/design capability is far from inconsequential. When compared to any single European country, firms from Japan have a larger share in consulting, feasibility (tied to evaluation of possible equity risks) and equipment supply — either independent or in consortium (Figure 5.2)

Companies from certain countries seem to be able to dominate particular project industry segments for specific kinds of services. The key to success seems to be in their ability either to contribute at the more complex end of the scale, or to provide exclusive technology.

124

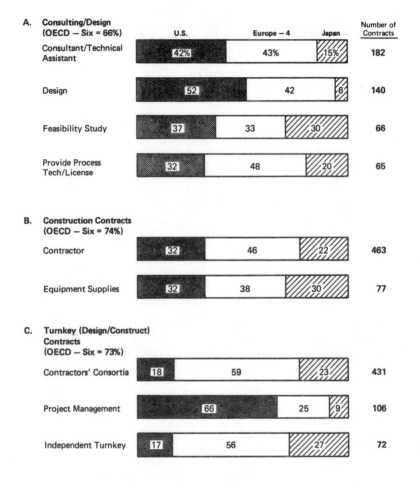

Figure 5.2

Modes of Technology Transfer
OECD - Six Breakdown

PROVIDING THE MISSING TECHNOLOGY

Excellence in service has the net result of creating a competitive advantage for the engineer or technology provider. The macroproject arena is composed of numerous service segments, and it is of interest to find that firms from certain countries seem to distinguish themselves because of their expertise — developed within their domestic market — which is in demand in Third World macroproject markets.

Process technology or other engineering expertise can be transferred to host sponsors by independent contracts for consulting, design, construction or equipment supply — or the entire process can be packaged by a group of companies in a contractors' consortium, or by a single lead company under an independent turnkey contract.

Consulting and Design Services

Companies who are successful in the developing world rely on their strong reputations and on expertise from their home countries as their entré into the macroproject arena. Since companies are not awarded contracts to diversify their services in the developing world, a clear track record of success is essential. There seem to be pockets of expertise that evolve in one country more than others. There are lots of big projects in the U.S. for example — and U.S. firms are often selected because of this and their experience in the developing world.

A case in point is the engineering requirements of major airport projects: 1) There are national airport specialists such as Aeroport de Paris (France), British Airport International (UK), NACO (The Netherlands), Italairport (Italy) which provide consulting or design assistance to Third World airport ministeries, and also provide development assistance and training; 2) There are also expert consulting engineers with specialties in airport design, such as Alexander Gibb & Partner (UK), William Halcrow & Partner (UK), TAMS (US), and P.R.C. Harris (US), who consult to specialists involved in planning and designing the projects, as well as in supervising and evaluating tenders; 3) When projects are extremely complex, design/constructors can be found: such companies are Bechtel (US) and Ralph M. Parsons (US). They provide construction management services including design, engineering, procurement, and management of construction. Their unique contribution is in their ability to deal with high levels of complexity by means of highly sophisticated project management systems, worldwide procurement networks, etc.

It is not surprising, then, that once a certain level of complexity is reached there are only a small group of contractors who dominate within project industry/service sectors.

Consulting contracts are awarded largely to firms from Japan, the United Kingdom, and the United States, who together hold 75

126

percent of the OECD-six consultancy contracts on macroprojects. The U.S. consultants have twice the number of contracts, however the Japanese and English are more specialized (Figure 5.3A). While

Figure 5.3

Lead Consultant/Technical Assistants: U.S., U.K., Japan Portfolio Breakdown

A. Portfolio by Industry Mix

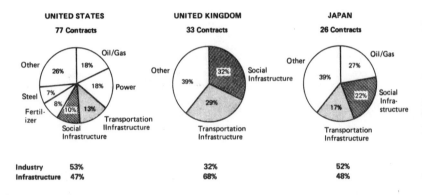

Industry	53%	32%	52%
Infrastructure	47%	68%	48%

B. Shares of Total Projects in Size Range

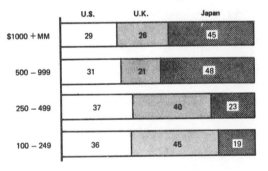

U.S. consultancies are diverse and serve all types of projects of all sizes, the Japanese have been winning the majority of consultancy contracts over $500 million investment, with the smaller projects being awarded to the United Kingdom. The Japanese' success with

Figure 5.4

U.S. Versus Non-U.S. Designers: Portfolio Comparisons

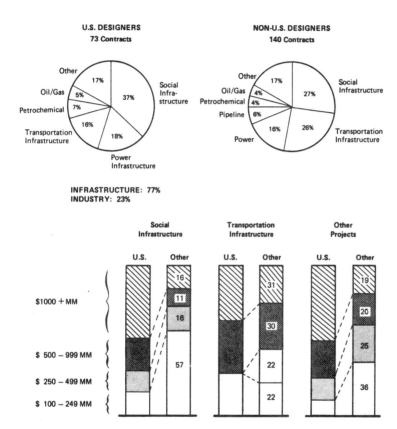

INFRASTRUCTURE: 77%
INDUSTRY: 23%

superb domestic rail and metro networks is providing them with leverage in winning railroad, mass transit, as well as port consultancy contracts at the international level. The British expertise is in social and transportation infrastructure (Figure 5.3B). They have been enormously active in the Middle East, particularly in consulting to port, harbor and housing projects.

Design contracts have been awarded to U.S. designers in one-third of the cases throughout the 1970s. Design contracts, as a separate award, usually involve design of an infrastructure facility,

128

although there are some such contracts in the hydrocarbon processing area.   Except for transportation infrastructure, the U.S.
dominates on most projects involving an investment of greater than
$500 million (Figure 5.4). The new capital city in Lagos, Nigeria,
and the Itaipu hydroelectric power plant in Brazil/Argentina are two
examples of projects designed by U.S. companies. In addition, U.S.
companies hold 42 percent of all design contracts associated with
social infrastructure, that is, housing complexes, educational institutions, hospitals, and other public buildings.

Process Technology Services

Contracts that include a process technology are frequently
awarded with the engineering and design component included in the
total contract.   Companies are bidding for these jobs either
independently or in consortium.

Independent turnkey contracts are generally for single units on
industrial projects below $500 million. These independent turnkey

Figure 5.5

**Europe-4 Versus Other
Independent Turnkey Contracts:
Portfolio Comparison**

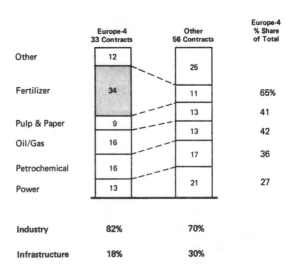

contracts are used largely on industrial projects. Most of the companies involved have an expertise in one unit of a processing facility, and under this contract, they agree to install that unit in total — from design to process, procurement and installation. One-third of these contracts have been awarded to European companies from the four most active countries — Italy, France, West Germany, and the United Kingdom. These four countries have won two-thirds of these contracts for projects dealing with hydrocarbon pro-cessing — and more specifically, fertilizer (Figure 5.5). European companies have a 64 percent share of fertilizer contracts — representing a third of their overall portfolio.

The contractors' consortium packages all the components into a total bid package. Consortia are used on all types of projects, of all sizes. They are not peculiar to any particular size range (Table 5.1). European companies outnumber the U.S. and Japanese

Table 5.1

Breakdown of Contractors' Consortia By Project Industry Type, and Investment Size

Project Investment	Industry (221)	Infrastructure (383)
$1,000 + MM	16%	29%
500 - 999	17	20
250 - 499	16	11
100 - 249	51	39

companies by 3:1. Contractors' consortia can most frequently be found in the Middle East and North Africa (54 percent). Saudi Arabia, Iran, Algeria, Iraq, Turkey, and Egypt attract close to half of such contracts. Brazil and India account for 5 percent each. The reason for this high concentration in these areas is that they are making massive efforts to rapidly develop infrastructure — which is highly risky and difficult for local industries to coordinate alone — at the same time that they have numerous industrial development projects underway. (These eight countries are among the top ten in macroproject activity.)

Figure 5.6 indicates the project industries that use contrac-tors' consortia, the number of contracts won by the OECD-six, the

130

Figure 5.6

Contractors' Consortia Membership Breakdown

	OECD-Six Contracts	Membership breakdown	Total Contracts	OECD – Six as % Total
1. Power	99	24 W. Germ. | 23 Italy | 18 Fran. | 17 Japan | 15 U.S.A.	149	64
2. Social	44	32 U.S.A. | 27 Japan | 18 France | 23 Rest	77	57
3. Transport	39	38 U.K. | 21 Japan | 18 U.S.A. | 23 Rest	65	60
4. Petrochemical	30	47 West Germany | 17 U.S.A. | 17 Italy | 19 Other	33	91
5. Oil/Gas	23	61 Japan | 22 Italy | 17 U.S.A.	25	92
6. Pipelines	21	43 Italy | 24 U.S.A. | 19 Japan | 14 Rest	25	84
7. Steel	18	61 Japan | 28 W. Germ. | 11 Rest	22	82
8. Fertilizer	16	50 West Germany | 19 Fran. | 31 Rest	22	73
9. Manufacturing: Other	12	67 Italy | 33 Rest	13	92
10. Communication	11	45 France | 36 U.S.A. | 19 Rest	12	92

membership composition by nationality, and the share of the total consortia contracts awarded represented by the OECD-six. One can see that the OECD-six are the most frequent initiators of the consortia approach. Most are pulled together to supply engineering and process technology to infrastructure projects, but petrochemical plants, oil refineries, steel mills and fertilizer plants are also frequently installed by these groups.

Some nationalities are more prominent in using consortia in one industry sector than the others. The West Germans take the lead in power plant installation (with the Italians), petrochemicals and fertilizer; the British lead in transport infrastructure; the Japanese in oil refinery and gas processing consortia; as well as steel mills; the Italians lead in pipeline construction and textile mills (manufacturing); and the French are the leaders in telecommunication installations.

More and more participants are exploring consortia as a mode of participation. Figure 5.7A shows the competitive dynamics that have been occurring in the power infrastructure sector over the last decade. By comparing currently completed projects with those under construction, and projects whose contracts have recently been let, one can see that over the last decade the use of consortia has expanded from usage by only the Italians and French, to usage by West Germany, the U.K., and the U.S. The Japanese increasingly are winning contracts in this sector. Compared to overall contract awards (Figure 5.7B), consortia participation as a percent of total contracts awarded has not changed. Consortia have consistently accounted for about sixty percent of the total.

Finally, one can observe the basis for increased competition for turnkey consortia — companies from developing countries and centrally planned economies, as well as Western European countries other than the OECD-six are increasingly winning consortia contracts (Figure 5.7C). Specifically, Canadian, Brazilian, and Swiss companies are significantly more active.

The consortia share outnumbers the independent project management contract by six to one, and is the most common way that an engineering/construction firm would find itself bidding for one of these jobs. Consortia and independent turnkey contracts are generally written on a fixed-fee basis, with the contractor absorbing most of the risks associated with delays or overruns. There are numerous variables that go into determining the optimum contractual formula. In general, the purpose of these packages is to take risk away from the host sponsors, and at the same time, take managerial control of construction out of the host sponsors' scope of direct daily responsibility.

Project Management Services

Project management contracts have been awarded to U.S. companies in two-thirds of the cases. U.S. companies have managed

132

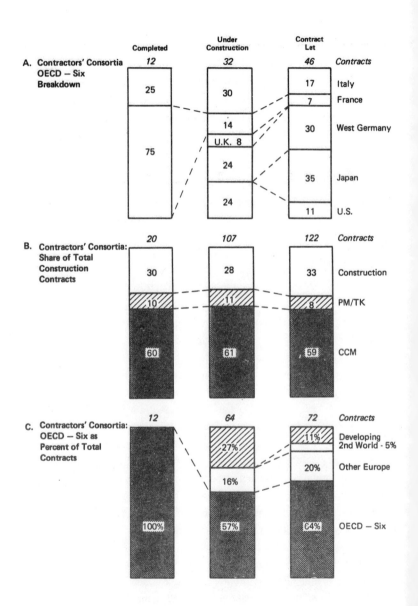

Figure 5.7

Power Infrastructure Development:
Trends in Collaboration

67 percent of the fertilizer projects and 82 percent of the oil refinery/LNG projects that required project management assistance (Figure 5.8A).

Figure 5.8

U.S. Versus Non-U.S. Project Managers:
Portfolio Comparisons

A. **Portfolio by Industry Mix**

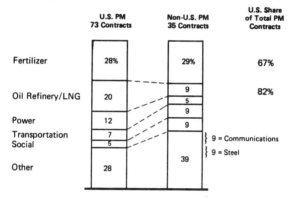

B. **Portfolio by Project Size**

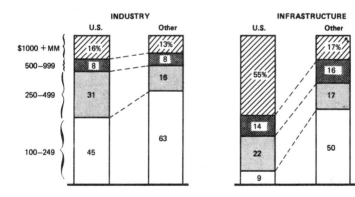

Analyzing the trend in contract awards by investment size, the U.S. firms have won a large percentage of industrial projects in the $250 to $499 million investment range, but otherwise, the mix is not distinctive from the other contractors. For infrastructure projects, however, 69 percent of the U.S. portfolio consists of projects of more than $500 million investment, compared to 33 percent for project managers of other nationalities (Figure 5.8B).

All projects of $1 billion or more requiring project management capabilities dealing with oil refineries, gas processing, and transportation infrastructure have been awarded to U.S. design/construction firms.

ENSURING SYNERGY IN DELIVERY

Multinational guests interested in winning a contract in the developing world put a lot of attention into preparing a competitive bid that skillfully balances quality against cost. It is not enough to measure one's success by number of contracts won, however. A technology supplier needs to assess the host's capabilities to determine if specific measures should be taken to anticipate possible coordination problems in the field.

It is not enough to win a bid — the technology contracted to be transferred must be installed in an effective way. Over the recent years, there has been a trend toward moving the project swiftly through its lifecycle from design to startup by ensuring that maximum cooperation is achieved 1) from one stage to another, 2) among processes installed, and 3) between host goals and multinational services. Achieving synergy among the many participants who have agreed to assist in the development process has been found to be critical. Effective project management, as well as strict team work, have been found to be essential to achieving the necessary coordination for a successful project.

Synergy in Management of Complexity

Managerial synergy is critical to coordinating grandscale undertakings. Macroprojects, whether industrial or infrastructure projects, are ambitious in scope and often entail several kinds of construction by multiple contractors who are undertaking their development activities at the same time. As discussed in Chapter 1, the most important opportunity for capitalizing on cost reduction opportunities, not to mention actively preventing overruns, lies in maximizing efficiencies during the construction phase. The ability to recognize and take immediate advantage of the trade-offs that occur daily can provide significant cost savings. In the macroproject arena, the need for managerial synergy is high on almost every project:

- On the $10 billion Ruweis Industrial Center, Fluor was overseeing the design and construction of an industrial park, port, new city, hospital, road and telecommunications network — any one of which would be a fair sized responsibility for any project manager. Assigned responsibility for managing the sequencing of this project by the owners, Fluor's project management authority included engineering, procurement, phasing of labor training and construction. The conflicts that invariably result from such a complex undertaking were anticipated and ironed out by delegating clear management authority to someone with proven project control experience.

- On a similar sized New City south of Riyadh in Saudi Arabia more than twelve consortia bid for the job — recognizing the high risk involved in such an undertaking. These separate consortia packages will need to be coordinated and sequenced.

- On the $900 million Soroako Nickel Mine and Refinery, International Nickel, the majority shareholder, was providing the nickel technology. Logistics were difficult. The project was on a green-site: A road, highway, housing, irrigation system, etc. were necessary. Because of the complexity, the project management responsibility was delegated to the contractor. First Dravo, and then Bechtel, were hired as project managers to coordinate the project activity.

Sometimes smaller companies seek macroproject contracts. Synergy can be achieved by working with partners who together will add up to the management and skill requirements of the project. The Finn-Iran contractors is an example: Four Finnish companies formed a consortium and won a contract to build a $170 million housing project near Tehran. Without strict internal management they would have been unable to assume such a responsibility.

Synergy in Process Technology Supply

The fertilizer industry is perhaps the most concentrated industry in terms of the small number of companies winning macroproject contracts. Ammonia, urea, gas processing, and sometimes nitric acid units must be sourced from international chemical engineering firms — each of whom is a specialist in only one unit of technology. Yet these firms must install the various parts in a way that will result in an integrated and efficient total system. Additionally, the sponsors must feel comfortable with its operational systems and procedures. This can require considerable training of the operating staff. The transfer process thus involves more than the sum of the processing design and equipment in the hands of the multinational guests. The real leaders in this industry do not merely provide their technological know-how — they also structure their contribution in a way that provides the managerial capabilities to integrate the parts into a cohesive, efficient whole. This synergy can be achieved in a number of ways: 1) by use of project management contracts (U.S. firms have 65 percent of these contracts); 2) by use of the contractors' consortia (West German firms have 50 percent of these); and 3) by use of independent turnkey contracts (Four Western European countries have 34 percent of these).

As an example, one can observe the portfolios of the two lead providers of ammonia technology — Pullman Kellogg and Uhde — Pullman participates frequently as project manager responsible for supervising construction of other units besides just ammonia, while Uhde uses the consortium as its vehicle for achieving the same level of coordination (Figure 5.9). This trend is supported by similar

Figure 5.9

Transferring Ammonia Technology:
Lead Companies

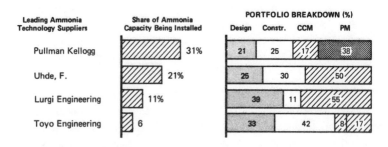

100% = 30,771 kty

trends in the oil refinery industry. One can see a share shift from companies supplying technologies with management capabilities, to design-constructors who select among a variety of available technologies. Fluor and Foster Wheeler, in particular, are known for their cost-plus project management capabilities which, though more expensive, are obviously addressing an important concern of host sponsors (Figure 5.10). Host organizations may be undecided about

Figure 5.10

**Oil Refinery Construction:
Share Trends of Technology Suppliers**

Share of Refinery Capacity Being Installed
by Current Status of Project

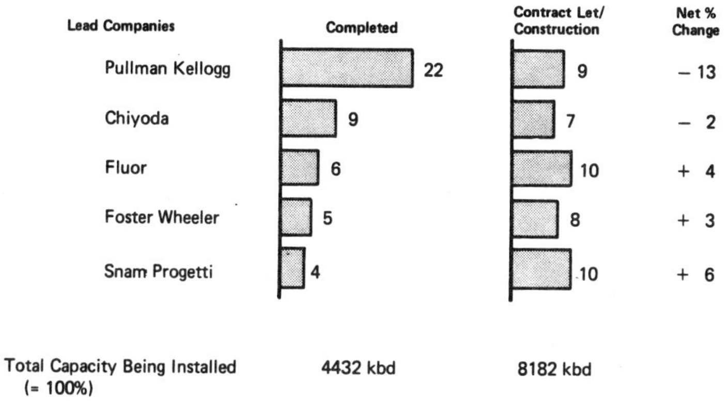

Lead Companies	Completed	Contract Let/ Construction	Net % Change
Pullman Kellogg	22	9	− 13
Chiyoda	9	7	− 2
Fluor	6	10	+ 4
Foster Wheeler	5	8	+ 3
Snam Progetti	4	10	+ 6
Total Capacity Being Installed (= 100%)	4432 kbd	8182 kbd	

the most appropriate technology, given the needs and peculiar characteristics of their country or resources. Such firms are able to determine the most appropriate technology. They are also able to coordinate the complex procurement process, source services from multiple suppliers, and provide quality checks and project control on the entire undertaking for the owners. They are also capable of training the construction and operating staffs and starting up the facility.

Synergy Between Consultants/Designers and Constructors

The turnkey approach — whether independent, as a project manager, or in consortium — makes this bridge between engineering and construction quite effectively. On projects where the turnkey

138

approach is not used, effective transfer of the design plan to the contractors — and their effective implementation of it — is critical. In one approach consultants and designers influence the selection of the constructors in favor of companies from their native country who are familiar with their working approach, specifications, etc. In practice, some contractor nationalities have a closer interface with consultants/designers from their home country than others. The West Germans are most likely to work with fellow constructors, the British are more likely to pass contracts to constructors from other countries (Figure 5.11).

Figure 5.11

**Interface Between Consultant and
Contractor by Country of Origin**

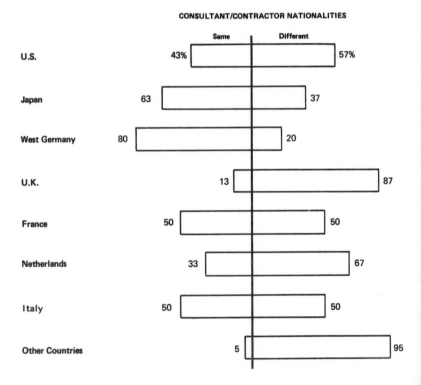

Some examples of how this works follow:

- On the Mantar I Hydroelectric project in Peru, Electro-consult (Italy) and Electrowatt (Switzerland) were the consultants, while Impregilo and GIE (both of Italy) constructed the plant in consortium.

- On the $1.2 billion Pohang Steel mill in South Korea, Nippon Steel (Japan) was the technical consultant to the owner and Nippon Kokan (Japan) was the contractor.

- On the Karakaya Dam in Turkey, Electrowatt (Switzerland) was the consulting engineer, along with others; TAMS — the U.S. design consortium — did the design; and Sulzer, Echer Wyss and Brown, Boveri — all of Switzerland — did the construction in consortium.

Other linkages of this type might exist between those that do feasibility and those who win the design contracts; or between the joint venture partners and engineers and constructors from their home countries, etc.

Synergy through the Contractors' Consortium

Like the resource consortium discussed in Chapter 4, the contractors' consortium divides project tasks among member companies who share both risks and rewards. The contract binding the members to the project is usually on a fixed-fee basis, negotiated by joint bidding organized by a lead participant, and backed by official export credit subsidies and/or government loans. This approach allows the potential members to determine the appropriate membership based upon the optimum mix of expertise required to meet project requirements. Since the sponsor(s) expect the contractors' consortium to see the project through the entire development process, consortia members have some independence in selecting partners who may contribute to one or more technology transfer tasks: 1) design and engineering; 2) procurement; 3) training; 4) construction; and 5) project coordination. However, in combination, all the required tasks must be covered.

Compatability of Consortia Members. In the macroproject sample there are four types of companies which can provide the contracted services: 1) engineering/construction companies (present on 69 percent of all consortia); 2) equipment manufacturers (present on 23 percent); 3) resource companies (24 percent); and 4) trading

140

Table 5.2

Contractors' Consortia Member Organizations And Potential Contribution to Macroproject Management

Project Management Responsibilities	Engineer/ Construction (E/C)	Equipment Manufacturer	Resource Company	Trading Company
Plant design and engineering	Plant design and engineering	Some design capability if turnkey	Plant design	Bring together the right companies
Procurement	Specify, select, and purchase	Supply equipment	Specify, select and purchase	Procure and manage logistics internationally
Training	Train construction staff and possibly operating staff	Train operating staff in home office when necessary		Arrange training of staff
Construction	Construct and staff	Possibly construct		Bring together the right companies
Project coordination/management	Supervise or manage construction	Manage if completely familiar with design	Coordinate if own technology	Coordinates on occasion but generally lacks technical background

companies (4 percent). The potential contributions which they can make to a macroproject are outlined in Table 5.2. In general, engineering/construction companies include 1) consulting/ design engineering firms, which take care of the plant design and engineering; 2) constructors, who only construct; and 3) design/ constructors, who can provide all services including project management. A consortium of these companies might include a mix of any or all of these. Equipment manufacturers typically become involved in a consortium to sell their technology process, including equipment. They may have engineers on their staff who provide design capability. They may or may not install the equipment. Oil, petrochemical, or metal companies may have process technologies they have developed which they are willing to sell on a contractual basis. Trading companies make their strongest contribution in the procurement and logistics area, as they have worldwide marketing networks to locate and evaluate bids.

The most common type of contractors' consortium is composed of engineering/construction companies only (34 percent). The next most common team also includes equipment manufacturers (20 percent) (Figure 5.12). The advantage of these combinations is that

Figure 5.12

The Contractors' Consortium:
Alternatives for Membership Composition by Type of Company

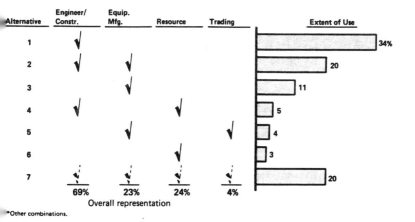

*Other combinations.

142

they permit a group of companies with complementary technologies — for example, the Araucaria Fertilizer plant in Brazil
(Table 5.3), to package their skills and resources in a way that

Table 5.3

**Engineering/Construction Companies As Contractors' Consortia
Members: Complementary Responsibilities**

Araucaria Fertilizer Plant, Brazil

Consortium Members	Project Responsibilities
Uhde	Provide ammonia technology Build ammonia unit
Lurgi	Install gas production and purification system
Stamicarbon	Provide urea technology Build urea unit

enables them to provide a complete facility with maximum
coordination and minimum involvement and risk to the host. In this
case, Uhde (West Germany) provided the ammonia technology and
built that unit; Lurgi (West Germany) installed the gas production
and purification system; and Stamicarbon (The Netherlands) provided the urea technology and installed that unit.   A further
example of this complementary mix of responsibilities can be seen
in the Italian consortium formed to install the Sumed pipeline — a
team of engineering/construction companies and equipment manufacturers (Table 5.4).   Snamprogetti did the overall project engineering; Chimi did the terminal and storage engineering; Italsider
and Montubi supplied the pipes; and Saipem managed the project
and carried out the construction.   While each company will be
involved at a different phase of the project, and their contributions
are exclusive, together they have built up a package which requires
minimal involvement by the host sponsor.

The ultimate purpose of all this mixing and matching is to end
up with a service advantage which the consortium can provide to the
host sponsors' macroproject.   Sometimes the link up with a host

Table 5.4

**Engineering/Construction Companies and Equipment
Manufacturers As Contractors' Consortia Members:
Complementary Responsibilities**

Sumed Pipeline, Algeria	
Consortium Members	Project Responsibilities
Snamprogetti	Project engineer
Chimi	Terminal and storage engineering
Italsider	Supplier of onshore pipes
Montubi	Supplier of offshore pipes
Saipem	Project manager, construction

company can provide the greatest leverage, as familiarity with the
local environment can provide the biggest cost and time savings on
one of these macroprojects. Table 5.5 traces some service
advantages provided by three consortia participating on projects in
Brazil.

Ansaldo Meccanico Nucleare went one step beyond the typical
consortium contract on one of their bids in the Middle East. They
not only provided technicians to train workers in local firms to carry
out a substantial portion of the construction job, but also developed
a local staff to run the completed plant. Plant staffing needs for
the completed project are often neglected on turnkey projects.

Benefits of National Consortia. OECD governments frequently
provide highly competitive financing to consortia activities as a
means of stimulating local industry. Not all consortia are formed
in order to meet the needs of a particular project. A significant
proportion of the consortia in a representative sample of macroprojects are composed of companies of a single nationality who
joined efforts at the behest, and with the support, of their own
government.

Throughout Europe, there are a number of permanent national
consortia that reorient and regroup to meet the changing requirements of various projects. Examples are Technip in France, and

Table 5.5

Service Advantages of Contractors' Consortia: Examples

Format	Example	Comparative Advantage
Engineering/construction companies; equipment manufacturers (host companies including guest companies with subsidiaries in the host country)	$248 million hydro plant Palmer Rio Negro, Brazil 8 Brazilian companies; Engevix; Montreal Engineering; Mechanica Peseda; General Electric; Ishibias	These companies knew the country. Were able to split tasks three ways, – Design – Equipment: turbines, generators – Hydromechanical equipment and transformers
Engineering/construction companies (guest/host)	$203 million Uberera Petrochem Plant, Brazil National Fluor (United States) Consultores Projectos (Brazil)	– Provides consortium access to local engineers, labor, training – Decreases likelihood of design errors by using experienced local talent
Equipment manufacturing (guest/host)	$707 million Itaipu Hydroelectric (segment), Brazil Mechanica Pesada (Brazil) (controlled by Schneider, France) Bardella (Brazil) (18 turbine generators)	Although the consortium had other competitive advantages, the inclusion of Bardella, a leading Brazilian owned manufacturer of capital goods swung the decision to its favor (it bid against a GE and a Westinghouse consortium)

Italimpianti and Snamprogetti in Italy. Since these and similar consortia have a reputation for their packaging of design and construction skills for the host country, they rarely seem to have trouble finding contracts on which to bid. If, in addition, they can obtain home-government financing support, they have a valuable competitive advantage over other potential bidders.

Motives for their home countries to provide this support include: 1) a desire to stimulate export to eliminate under-utilization of capacity; 2) reinforce intergovernmental relations; and 3) secure raw material supplies in exchange for technology. The benefits of home-country financing usually flow in two directions. For example:

- The Italian national contractors' consortia have been particularly aggressive in preparing low bids to win contracts in Middle Eastern countries. On the home front, they need to utilize excess manufacturing capacity to maintain employment levels; internationally, they need to earn foreign exchange used to meet their energy needs and to stabilize relations with oil suppliers. Although their low bids make them vulnerable to unchecked inflation that can impact their already tight margins and scarcity of materials, due to overloaded port conditions in the host countries where they are active, the state-owned banks and insurance companies in Italy are standing behind these endeavors, insuring the consortium members against potential difficulties. Thus, the members can satisfy some of their own country's needs while giving their Mideast hosts an attractive package.
- Similarly, the Canadian national contractors' consortium formed to construct the Gilan Pulp and Paper complex on the Caspian Sea in Iran is making an array of benefits available for home and host alike. Under the leadership of Stadler Hurter of Montreal, and supported by a Canadian chartered bank consortium and the Export Development Corporation of Canada, the consortium is providing:
  - Procurement contracts ($50 million) for 300 Canadian suppliers
  - A construction contract ($50 million) for a joint venture company composed of a Montreal firm and three Iranian construction firms

— Training for approximately 2,000 Iranians who will manage the complex when the Canadians depart.

It should be noted that in the U.S. the Webb-Pomerene Act of 1918 permits only exporters of goods to cooperate in formulating export bids. Extension of this privilege to providers of services is under active consideration in Congress. Currently, exporters can always "merely" cooperate, but they cannot engage in cartelized activity or competitive bidding or pricing.

Third World governments are not inactive in assisting their nationals in obtaining macroproject business.

- The Philippines government, for example, has formed a permanent consortium of 23 local contractors, called Filipino Contractors International, in order to improve wage and work agreements on foreign projects.

- An innovative variation was devised by the Brazilian government. It agreed to provide low interest financing to a $15 billion international contractors' consortium of American, French, and Saudi partners bidding on a Saudi Arabian project, provided that the host agreed to employ 20,000 Brazilian laborers on the project.

Benefits of International Consortia. In contrast to government-backed consortia, international consortia seem to be motivated almost entirely by economic or commercial factors. Companies seriously committed to project business seldom hesitate to cross national boundaries in quest of partners who can help sharpen the consortium's competitive edge. The international sourcing of partners enables consortia members to achieve maximum synchronization of complementary skills and financial resources.

Although U.S. firms have been unable to compete as a national consortium against the elaborate packages assembled in Europe and Japan they have been actively participating in international consortia. An example is the Joint Venture Qattara, formed to carry out the Qattara Depression Hydroelectric Power project in Egypt (Table 5.6). Harza Engineering of the U.S. teamed up with Salzgitter, Deutsche Project and Lahmeyer International, all of West Germany, to design and install this hydroelectric facility. Harza Engineering's expertise made them an attractive and equal partner with the Germans. For Harza, access to West German government project subsidies was made possible.

147

Table 5.6

International Contractors' Consortium: Qattara Depression Hydroelectric Project, Egypt.

Joint Venture Qattara		
Member Company	Country	Type
Salzgitter Consulting Company	West Germany	Engineer/constructor
Deutsche Project	West Germany	Electrical equipment manufacturer
Lahmeyer International	West Germany	Engineer/constructor
Harza Engineering	United States	Engineer/constructor

A sample of representative macroprojects shows that 48 percent of all contractors' consortia are composed of companies from the same country.   One-third are a mixture of multiple nationalities.   The host is a partner on 17 percent of these consortia (Figure 5.13).

Figure 5.13

**The Contractors' Consortium:
Alternatives for Membership by Country of Origin**

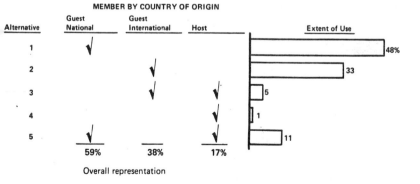

The mix of members by nationality has implications for the type of contribution the consortium is capable of making to the

Table 5.7

Contractors' Consortia Member Nationalities And Potential Contribution to a Macroproject

Project Requirements	National Guests	National Guests And Host	International Guests	International Guests And Host	Hosts
Capital Sourcing	Home government financial backing	Home government financial	Benefit from multiple EXIM loans/credits	Benefit from multiple EXIM loans/credits	Home government financial backing
Technology transfer	Lower bids	Local content, local labor	More economic sourcing of skills/resources possible		Local content, local labor
Market access	Barter deal possible	Barter deal possible	Barter deal possible, but more difficult	Barter deal possible	

project. The main differences are that national consortia usually bring low-interest financing; host involvement usually fulfills local content/local labor requirements; while international partnerships might be stronger technologically or in terms of procurement or marketing (Table 5.7).

Achievable Financial Advantages. Many of these projects, particularly infrastructure, are eligible for concessionary financing by international organizations. Their loans seldom cover the total cost of the project, however. Many of these loans are not given when the approach selected is turnkey as, in these cases, the providers of concessionary financing would not have the authority to monitor construction. For other high risk resource development projects, equity shareholders bring with them a wide range of debt facilities. It is those projects that are ineligible for concessionary financing, not desirous of splitting equity, and with scarce foreign exchange that presents a real coordination problem for host sponsors and multinational guests alike. Increasingly, contractors are taking the initiative — with their governments — in providing supplier or buyer credits — whether from their export credit facilities, or through private banking arrangements. Bank lending — to the contractor, or as an advance to the host country for purchases to be made — does not provide the low interest advantages of government-sourced financing. A very small group of official export credit agencies/facilities provide a lion-share of this financial support to contractors: U.S. EXIM, Japan EXIM, Coface (France), and Hermes (West Germany).

Table 5.8 shows some examples of how consortia were used to provide financial advantages to consortia members, and ultimately, to the host sponsors who requested the bid. One way to cut costs is to bid jointly — on the $1.5 billion desalting plant in Saudi Arabia, five Japanese equipment manufacturers prepared a joint bid. They saved money by making joint estimates; they did not have to bid against each other; and they were able to bid on this very large project by sharing the risk.

Another way to achieve a financial advantage is to link up with the host. On a bid for the $15 billion Al Assard Missile City in Saudi Arabia, Sam P. Wallace, as U.S. construction company, built up a consortium with a Brazilian partner, Noberto Odebrecht; a Saudi partner, Gharith P. Pharaon; a fellow American, 3-D

Table 5.8

Financial Advantages of National Contractors' Consortia: Examples

Format	Example	Competitive Advantage of Consortium Arrangement
Equipment manufacturers (national)	$1.5 billion desalting plant, Saudi Arabia Five Japanese equipment manufacturers	- Reduces cost of making estimates and preparing bids - Is able to bid on larger contracts by sharing risks - Eliminates bidding against each other
Engineer/construction (international, host and other Third World)	$15 billion Al Assard Missile City, Saudi Arabia Sam P. Wallace Co. (U.S.) Construction; Noberto Odebrecht (Brazil); Sofretu (France); 3-D International (United States); Gharith R. Pharaon (Saudi)	- Can cut extremely high risks by going to cheapest sources of financing (e.g., Brazilian government financing) - Reduces labor costs because Brazilian government will provide bonds and performance guarantees, as well as recruit and train 20,000 Brazilians for the project

International; and a French partner, Sofretu. They were able to cut the extremely high risks by accessing very cheap financing from the Brazilian government in exchange for training 20,000 Brazilians who would work on the project — with Brazilian government bonds and performance guarantees.

ANTICIPATING POTENTIAL PROBLEM AREAS

The attraction of the turnkey approach is that project owners need not worry about the technical, managerial, and risk components of project development — except in those cases where a cost-plus contract or is retained (then it is advisable for the owner to, at a minimum, monitor the project). It is true that the project management contract is awarded because the owners do not have the experience or inhouse capability to manage the project themselves and/or lack familiarity with installation of the technology. Nevertheless, the owners are expected to have some kind of procedures to review and approve the designs and requisitions of the contractor. The signature by the host is a requirement on all cost-plus transactions.

It is important to examine how successful these contractors have been in fulfilling their contractual commitments in the 1970s — a highly turbulent and high-risk period.

1. Turnkey contracts do become more vulnerable to trouble as the project becomes more complex. The percent of all projects with these contracts that experience cost escalations, completion delays or postponements does increase directly with increase in project size (Table 5.9). The project management contract is usually cost-plus, making incidence of trouble more visible.

2. Turnkey contracts vary in the degree of overruns and delays by industry sector. The contractors' consortium fares best in fertilizer, petrochemicals, social and transport infrastructure, and steel projects, but there are some overruns near 100% and delays of 3 to 4 years in oil refinery, LNG and power projects. The project management contractors have records of huge overruns on certain aluminum and power projects; and delays of about 1 year on many projects. The independent turnkey contractor, usually less vulnerable to troubles than the project

152

Table 5.9

**Breakdown of Turnkey Contracts by Type,
Project Size ($ Millions) and Trouble Rate**

Turnkey Type	% of Total Per Size Range With Trouble			
	$100–249	$250–499	$500–999	$1,000+
Contractors' Consortium	24%	24%	33%	44%
Project Management	34	52	50	83
Independent Turnkey	30	21	66	50

manager because contingency estimates are included in his
bids, also has a better track record: a maximum 60
percent overrun and few if any delays.

3. The major turnkey contractors are quite effective in their
control of macroprojects. Since the hydrocarbon processing industries are the most concentrated, the averages
of their worst case experiences in macroproject development are illustrated (Figure 5.14). Their overall track
record is quite favorable, with trouble they encountered
running lower than those for the total project segment
(see Chapter 4).

4. Nationality mix is not an important factor when it comes
to selecting partners for a contractors' consortium (Table
5.10).

Table 5.10

**Nationality of Contractors' Consortia Members and
Trouble Rate**

Consortium Composition	Trouble Rate
Guest national only	34%
Guest and host national	38
International guests	42
International guests and host	41

Figure 5.14

Summary of Trouble Experienced
By Major Contractors by Type of Involvemei.

INDUSTRY / COMPANY	CONSORTIUM		TURNKEY		PROJECT MANAGEMENT	
	CE	CD	CE	CD	CE	CD
OIL REFINERY						
Bechtel (U.S.)	36%	3 y.s.	33%	1	0	0
Chiyoda (Japan)	36	4	0	0	0	0
Fluor (U.S.)	0	0	33	1	58	1
Foster Wheeler (U.S.)	0	0	0	0	0	2.5
Ishikawajima H. Hvy (Japan)	36	0	0	0	0	0
Itoh, C. (Japan)	36	0	0	0	0	0
Japan Gasoline Ltd. (Japan)	36	0	0	0	0	2
Pullman-Kellogg (U.S.)	156	0	0	0	10	0
Mitsubishi (Japan)	0	4	75	1	0	0
Snam Progetti (Italy)	− 9	3	4	1	0	0
PETROCHEMICALS/CHEMICALS						
Bechtel (U.S.)	0	0	0	0	150	6
Fluor (U.S.)	18	0	0	0	29	4
Kellogg Continental (U.S.)	0	0	0	0	0	0
K-H-D (W.G.)	12	7	0	0	0	0
Lummus, C.E. (U.K.)	19	0	0	0	173	3
Montecatini-Edison (Italy)	0	0	260	4	0	0
Snam Progetti (Italy)	0	0	0	0	0	0
Technip-KTI (French)	0	0	67	3	0	0
Uhde, Friedrich (W. Germany)	9	0	0	4	0	0
PETROCHEMICALS/FERTILIZER						
Fluor (U.S.)	0	0	0	0	26	0
Foster Wheeler (U.S.)	14	0	0	0	0	0
K-H-D (W. Germany)	0	0	0	0	0	0
Lurgi (W. Germany)	−32	1	0	0	0	0
Mitsubishi (Japan)	0	0	0	0	0	0
Mitsui Toatsu Chem. (Japan)	0	0	0	0	0	0
Pullman-Kellogg (U.S.)	0	0	−11	0	9	1
Snam Progetti (Italy)	0	0	0	0	30	2
Stamicarbon (Neth)	0	0	0	0	0	0
Technip-KTI (French)	0	0	0	0	0	0
Topsoe (Denmark)	0	1	0	0	0	0
Toyo Eng. Corp. (Japan)	0	2	0	0	15	1
Uhde, Friedrich (W. Germany)	−32	0	21	0	0	0

Although roughly 40 percent of the consortia in the sample have experienced some kind of trouble, the magnitude of the overruns or delays are actually quite low.

In summary, the engineering/construction arena in the developing world is highly segmented and diversified, and requires highly sophisticated appraisal of technological gaps and potential pitfalls in delivery. The winners are those who are able to capitalize on their expertise and position in their home country in providing technological and financial support to host-sponsored macroprojects.

A smooth collaboration of these companies with the owners is essential to effective management. The next chapter discusses a range of options to effectuate such coordination.

6
Effective Project Control

The real opportunity for macroproject sponsors to influence the success or failure of their projects lies in preserving their overall integrity throughout the development phase — that is, in faithfully implementing the project according to the original definition as conceived in the early planning, feasibility and engineering phases. Since enormous volumes of capital and resources are expended during the construction phase, maximizing efficiencies at that critical period, in particular, can make the difference between loss or profit to the sponsors. The challenge lies in ushering the project swiftly and surely through the engineering, procurement, construction, and startup phases with minimal budget and schedule deviations.

Not every project requires a project manager. A project warrants such a lead decision-maker — that is, an active capability to make timely trade-off decisions — when it is highly complex, whether in a technological, political, logistical, or financial sense. The project manager conveys pertinent status information and trade-off options to onsite and headquarters managers, owners and other interested officials on a routine basis. He interprets the numerous computer outputs and statistical analyses to identify signals of impending trouble. An effective project management capability serves the function of providing an "early-warning" system. The project manager makes the necessary compromises and adjustments as soon as possible to minimize the time and cost impact of the trouble on the project.

Project management expertise may be provided by any of a number of qualified sources including the owners themselves, or international design/construct firms. Services retained from international firms are usually reimbursed on a cost-plus-fee contractual basis. The project management contractor (PMC) is normally selected because of the sophistication of his tracking systems, his relevant experience in installing the particular technology, and/or his proven record in dealing with projects of a similar level of complexity. Previous experience in the country can also be enormously valuable.

This chapter focuses on how the optimum control system for a particular macroproject is determined. There is no single ideal way of structuring the management and control system of a macroproject to ensure its success. Careful evaluation must be made of the skills and talents of the owners and prospective project managers; the requirements of the particular project; and the web of social, cultural, political, and logistical issues that surround the project and add to its complexity. From the survey of macroprojects in the 1970s it is possible to identify the main project components which must be linked organizationally in order for the project's overall integrity to be preserved; what the role of the owner is in project control; and what the real parameters are of the project manager's responsibilities.

PRESERVING PROJECT INTEGRITY

The decision to establish a formal control system as well as to determine how extensive that system should be depends upon who has been selected to develop the project and what their commonality is with respect to the goals and perspectives of the owners. The owners must be able to recognize at all times that the project is on course. Their project is in control when its current progress is in clear harmony with the specific objectives set out at the beginning of the project, that is, the appropriate amount of human, capital or material resources have been expended within the predicted timeframe to achieve the desired results. The project's progress can be effectively tracked when 1) all responsibilities are clearly defined; 2) there are mechanisms for recording time and resource expenditures; and 3) there is a management organization capable of interpreting changed circumstances and of identifying situations that require timely trade-off decisions.

Overall, owners should not hesitate to retain a project management contractor should they be inexperienced in managing a project of such complexity or if they are unfamiliar with the technology. Nevertheless, the owners should not abandon the project to the PMC. When the project manager is not one of the owners, it becomes important to establish some objective checks and balances over the PMC. It is the owners who bear the rewards or penalties for the ultimate success or failure of a macroproject — except in the cases where the contractors are retained on a fixed fee basis, in which instance they bear the cost of any overrun. On a cost-plus contract, it is advisable for the owners to be involved in monitoring the implementation of the contract.

On a continuum from high control to no control, the level of organization that must be developed to monitor the project manager depends on whether the owner and project manager have certain perspectives in common or whether the owners must set up an organizational linkage with the PMC to make input into his decisions. The presence or absence of certain linkages surfaces guidelines for an optimum organizational structure for controlling a macroproject.

1. Risk and Responsibility: The integrity of the project is more likely to be preserved when there is an organizational connection between those who bear the financial risks and those who wield management responsibility during the development of the project. Owners assume the financial risks, the project management contractors do not. If the project exceeds the budget and schedule parameters — that is, if it goes out of control — the owners are the ones who bear the loss. The project will have to be refinanced, at a minimum, and it may even cause the project to lose its economic viability vis-a-vis competitive projects in the industry. Because of the cost-plus nature of the PMC's contract, they are not vulnerable to any financial penalties should any complications arise. Monitoring by the owner assures that a common level of diligence in meeting cost and budget commitments is exerted.

2. Developmental and Operational Objectives: The integrity of the project is more likely to be preserved when there is an organizational connection between those who are committed to the viability of the operating facility and

those who are committed to the technological challenges of developing the project. As a project is implemented, there are numerous unexpected adaptations to the original concept that must be made, particularly if the project involves a new technology, or a technology that must be specifically tailored to the mineral being extracted or processed. Owners are committed to the project because of its potential as an operating facility. PMCs are committed to the project because of its technological challenge. From an operational perspective, the completed facility will need to compare favorably with other existing facilities in the domestic and global industry. Owners probably have the clearest perception of where the trade-offs between quality and cost should be made. The conscientious PMC appreciates this reality, and requires owner approval on all design and procurement as standard operating procedure. Left to his own devices, a PMC would like to install the most technologically excellent facility, at whatever the cost. Since most lead project managers are typically engineers, this type of professional motivation is instinctive and should be respected and anticipated. By monitoring the PMC, the owners can be sure that the PMC has an accurate perception of the job, that their quality control standards are acceptable and at the right level, and that they have assigned the best staff for the task at hand. The owner typically tracks the PMC by means of a project team, committee, or by assigning a single representative.

3. Sources and Uses of Financial Resources: The integrity of the project is more likely to be preserved when there is an organizational connection between those who supply financing to the project and those who disburse the capital to suppliers, workers, etc. Enormous amounts of capital are committed to these macroprojects. Using the capital in the most productive way throughout the development of the project can provide numerous opportunities to maximize returns on the money. Owners are concerned with the project from a cash management point of view. Whoever manages the project focuses logistically, from a

cash disbursement perspective. Whether the owner provides the financing himself, or obtains financing from lenders, he must be up-to-date on the amount of cash to be made available, capital to be reinvested until required, and new capital that must be sourced to cover overruns. These needs require careful assessment by the owner, based on information developed through the project tracking system. In contrast, the project manager is concerned with identifying expenses and wages that require reimbursement. He looks at cost, schedule, materials flow, materials received, from a logistical, rather than a purely financial perspective.

4. Developers and Developees: The integrity of the project is more likely to be preserved when there is an organizational connection between those who are developing the project and those who surround the project and will benefit or be disturbed by its impact. The environment that surrounds a macroproject can present as serious an impediment to progress as any technological or logistical factor. Of all the players, a host owner is probably the most effective in establishing smooth ties with government officials and ministeries as well as with the local communities bordering the project. An international project management contractor, on the other hand, brings expertise in worldwide procurement of goods and engineering services, training and development of indigenous labor forces, and sequencing efficiency in managing the flow of goods and materials. When the internal capability of the owners includes these capabilities, the PMC may not be necessary. On the other hand, the PMC has the competence to develop the entire project independently, should the host sponsor lack all or any of these competencies. Any project control organization should include structural capability to deal with players surrounding the project.

In summary, as the owners move toward delegating more and more control to the independent PMC, they should develop a more extensive organizational structure to make a linkage with the PMC in the area where decisions are made that are of special concern to the owners. All owners, regardless of level of equity, should be able to follow developments as they occur, and make input, when appropriate, to key decisions. Nevertheless, project managers should be given sufficient authority to act quickly and surely. They should be monitored, but they should not be bogged down in numerous debates about how they could have made better trade-offs, or in reporting to or requiring approval of every decision from cumbersome committees. Communications do need to be established. However, bureaucratization of communication should not be permitted to occur. Flexibility is critical to fighting the numerous daily "fires" that arise in the most expedient way.

The next section describes how these features of the owner/PMC relationship impact the way a macroproject is organized to manage and control the development phase.

THE ROLE OF THE OWNER

The owner's objective in establishing an organizational framework is to enable each participant to know what to expect from the others, how to handle the differences of opinion, how to reach decisions, how to keep the project moving. Real cooperation must be achieved. Decision-making must be done swiftly and surely, giving prime consideration to the status of the project, rather than to that of the person who sits across the table.

A review of existing macroprojects indicates that there are three generic ways in which owners structure their projects. The level of owner involvement is a function of a given owner's degree of experience or competence in pursuing the project independently. An owner can:

1. Actively manage. Undertake the project itself — either as a sole host organization, or through a joint venture.

2. Direct and control. Contract out the project preparation to consulting or design engineers and/or construction work to contractors.

3. Review and approve. Contract out the complete job to either a project manager, turnkey contractor, or consortium. In the case of turnkey projects, managerial or supervisory control is delegated to the contractor who supplies a complete package at a fixed fee, thus assuming any risk involved.

Actively Manage

When the team of owners manages the project jointly, fully sharing responsibilities, separate monitoring or control checks are not needed. Risks are assumed by those who also wield control. The project tracking system and the control or monitoring system are one and the same.

- On the Maui LNG project, in New Zealand, Shell, BP and Todd (a local oil company) are equity partners, providers of technology and responsible for onsite supervision. Their joint venture organization tracks the budget and schedule for the project in its entirety. Foreign advisors are involved in technical discussions and quality assessment.

- On the Tubarao Steel project, Siderbras (the Brazilian steel company), Finsider (the Italian steel company), and Kawasaki Steel (Japan) each hold equity as well as decision-making responsibility for all phases of construction control and management via representation by each partner in all departments, committees, and on the Board of Directors of the joint venture company.

Direct and Control

In some cases, one of the joint venture partners may take the lead in directing the work of the PMC because of its strong technical expertise. That company will be delegated audit responsibility, as representative of the owners, in overseeing work of the project manager, and it will serve as the PMC's sole contact point in communicating with the project owners.

- On the Soroako Nickel project, International Nickel (INCO) of Canada did the preliminary engineering, worked with the project manager in devising a critical path computerized tracking system, and monitored the engineering progress from the headquarters office in Toronto. The other shareholders (Japanese — 5 percent) relied on INCO's tracking documentation to stay abreast of the project status. They required no other input or crosschecks.

- On the Bougainville Copper project, the joint venture metal companies worked out the preliminary engineering, geological and marketing assessment together, then audited the project manager's implementation of their plans during construction and startup via a project team. The Papua New Guinea government managed all of the political problems.

In some cases the owners may want to control the PMC; however, their own internal organizations may not be strong enough to adequately monitor the status of the project. They often hire engineers as members of a task force or as independent consultants who act as their agents in certain aspects of project control.

- On the Badak and Arun LNG projects, Pertamina wanted to maintain complete ownership but lacked the staff to monitor Bechtel, the cost-plus project management contractor. Bechtel had day-to-day decision-making authority in the field, but all of their work was approved. Pertamina hired experts from around the world (60 percent were foreign), as well as from the companies who were supplying the gas (Huffco Consortium — Badak; Mobil Oil — Arun) to staff their task force. Because the project was financed by the companies who agreed to purchase the output, another layer of control was built in by the Indonesian government who audited the finances.

- On the Krakatau Steel Mill project, the owner, Pertamina, set up an organization to manage the project, hired Kaiser to design the work packages and act as technical advisor, and contract out the jobs on a lump sum basis. The net effect of this "lump-sum" arrangement was that it shifted financial risk from the project to the contractors. In such a situation, owner control becomes both difficult and unnecessary. Kaiser performed quality checks and used payment for work completed as incentive to control the sequencing and timeliness of the individual contractors.

Review and Approve

When one equity partner is stronger technically than the others, this partner might assume lead project management responsibility, but controls are installed to satisfy the other risk-taker's concern that the most economical decisions are being taken.

- On the Asahan Aluminum project, a large Japanese consortium held 90 percent equity, however, Sumitomo Chemical was providing the smelter technology and thus undertook lead management responsibility. OECF, the Japanese government project financing organization, who was also a consortium member, strictly tracked all expenditures and reported back to the other shareholders.

- On the Sarawak LNG project in Malaysia, Shell serves as the provider of the technology, the production supplier of the gas to the LNG plant and will manage the operating company for the other partners — Petronas and Mitsubishi. Shell has not been given a free hand, however. The budget and schedule will be monitored by the joint venture organization and all policy decisions will be made by the Joint Board.

Inability to Control

Sometimes, owners have difficulty tracking a macroproject because of insufficient manpower or tracking systems. This can be detrimental to overall progress.

- On a multibillion dollar industrial development project — enormous in scope — the owners have a team of relatively inexperienced people who had no system for tracking and thus concentrated more on observing the PMC, rather than keeping their eye on the progress of the overall project. Because this was unfruitful, the project organization was rearranged. All of the owner's staff were integrated into the PMC organization — with the exception of the owner's project director. The top four managers of the owner in the integrated organization reported to two project directors. All the decision-making authority was channelled from the contractor's lead manager, after he negotiated with the client director. The contractor insisted that the owner continue to audit, however, because of the cost-plus nature of the contract and the financial exposure of the owner.

Other factors may occur during construction which might force a reorganization of the project control system. Sometimes the project moves from centralized to decentralized control as the project progresses. Sometimes the owners feel uncomfortable with the status reports received from their representative partner or the PMC and want to move to more of a committee approach — or conversely, to a more delegated approach. Typically, the desire to rearrange the organizational structure can be traced to an ineffective communication flow — either too little, or over-bureaucratized. Project momentum depends on the spirit of the law — not an overcommitment to counting the pennies. Nevertheless, both sides should feel comfortable that the goals are clear and shared and that the project is on track.

REAL PARAMETERS OF PROJECT MANAGEMENT

Many observers who admire the excellent project control exhibited by the U.S. space program wonder why the same level of expertise cannot be brought to bear on Third World macroprojects. In fact, macroprojects involve a host of intervening variables that are enormously more difficult to control than the physical and technological variables confronted in the space program. The project sponsors and managers engaged in macroprojects have the difficult task of trying to develop innovative ways to install technology in the midst of extensive social turbulence.

It is true that project management assistance is usually sought on projects with high economic or technical risks and/or when there are multiple plants and infrastructural pieces going on at the same time. The project manager ensures that the project keeps moving, that there is a timely flow of information that clarifies for the concerned parties the actual status of the project. An effective manager uses a combination of time-planning, cost control analysis, input/output models, etc. as a basis for interfacing with the owners and keeping them informed. The PMC can be made accountable for his performance through the establishment of cost centers. All layers of management and supervision can be held responsible for distinct pieces of the project through establishment of clear single-person authority lines.

Much attention has been given to the sophistication of the project manager's control system. In fact, without effective leadership — that is, someone with a strong and decisive personality to generate enthusiasm and a sense of direction — all of these tools are useless. The reason that this has been found to be important is that in addition to standard project tracking, sequencing and coordination responsibilities, project managers on macroprojects in the developing world have the added responsibilities of managing a variety of important and extremely divergent stakeholders. The prevalent requirement that local content and local labor be used as much as possible on these projects, for example, creates certain problems: Accessing sufficient quantities of local workers to meet the needs of the projects can be difficult. The large numbers of expatriates that must be brought onsite to manage the more technical aspects of the project require careful management. The intense nationalistic frictions that result from matching widely divergent staff together can present enormous problems.

Developing Trade Skills

The project manager is responsible for sourcing and training adequate quantity and quality of indigenous labor. Major U.S. PMCs, for example, work with the local governments in setting up training programs in all crafts, including welding, with the government often providing the training facility. A dearth of local technical expertise can be overcome by excellent training programs developed for the construction, as well as the operations, staff.

The PMC first forecasts the number of people needed per function, when they will be needed, and then commences the training accordingly. PMC's use three- and six-month introductory programs, as well as upgrading programs. The training is very demanding and continues as an on-going activity throughout the life of a project. It would be impossible to conduct on-the-job training without the initial training program, however, as the basic program provides the rudiments of the skill.

Some very able workers have been produced by these on-site programs. They are willing to work, eager, and, with proper direction — someone who displays sufficient interest — they have developed very fast. Given the proper work force, training, and good on-site conditions, some managers believe that they can raise productivity to the highest standards anywhere in the world.

To train the operating staff, two approaches are typically used: Either the trainee is assigned to an expatriate counterpart in the operating company, or he is sent to the headquarters of a joint venture partner in the U.S., Europe or Japan for training in an operating facility. Counterpart training can take three to seven years; training abroad can take six months to two years.

Some of the Badaks in the project discussed in Chapter 1 were sent to U.S. universities to study. Others were trained for four

months in welding and other construction skills. They were then
expected to perform at the same level of competence as a four-year
apprenticed U.S., European or Australian worker. Still others were
given two weeks of driving lessons, even though they had never seen
trucks before in their lives. A haul truck was worth a quarter of
a million dollars; if they had an accident, they would have to wait
a year for a new truck. The stakes were high. These, and other
daily trade-offs and quick and timely decisions must be made by the
project manager. A highly experienced project management
organization has been found to be particularly sharp in recognizing
and developing talent.

Creating an Expat Community

The expat staff can also present problems. The PMC
responsible for the expat staff must address problems associated
with life in a remote location in order to minimize turnover. The
key to solving these problems is to create a sense of community.

The layout of the town can play an important role in fostering
a sense of community. Two metal mining projects in Australia have
been innovative in this respect. In Kambalda, the houses were built
in the natural brush with old-fashioned terraces and an inner area
where the shops were located. No moving vehicles were permitted,
encouraging interaction and a sense of belonging. In Weipa, houses
were designed to take advantage of the breezes, but they had no
air-conditioning, although the town was hot and humid. Community
centers were provided with air-conditioning, so that wives would be
attracted to them and their sense of isolation would be reduced.

At a project in Papua, New Guinea, expats were not allowed
to create little Americas or Australias or Europes by clustering
together. The same type of housing was assigned to whites and to
blacks. The size of the house allotted to each person was
determined by the number of children in the family in Western
Australia. However, at Papua, house size depended upon the
position of the expat in the managerial heirarchy of the project.
They often shared the same level of responsibility with indigenous
managers. Certain categories of housing were indigenous houses —
very small and not meant for expats. Nevertheless, a lot of expats
were housed in them. This made a positive impression on the local
residents and fostered a feeling of collaboration.

Minimizing the "Company Town" Presence

Another problem that is all-pervasive is the constant presence of the company in a company town. When all the shops are owned by the company (usually the joint venture company of the owners) and the company must approve everything, there is a sense of "Big Brother" watching. Efforts at creating independent local industry, and at combining and mixing several company towns have been found to be effective in enriching these communities as well as in lowering the overall cost of infrastructure.

Managing Social Change

Numerous conflicts arise when macroprojects are situated near existing local communities, or when transmigration of large populations of local people is required. Problems often occur at the moment of site selection when indigenous people are removed from their land (such as the Bahasas mentioned in Chapter 1); and at the moment of startup when the number of jobs is sharply reduced, and unemployment sharply rises in the areas (such as the project in Sulawesi, also Chapter 1).

In between these starting and ending points there are numerous conflicts which invariably arise. Formal procedures for developing a satisfactory rapport with the community on an ongoing basis are needed. The most common approach for handling these cultural problems is to establish a local community development authority that will interface with the tribal chiefs and indigenous people throughout the development of the project. A foreign owner or contractor ideally should never be directly involved in these sometimes very emotional transactions. Local participants are better able to appreciate the delicacy of these sudden changes on community life.

The creation of a sense of involvement in the project is important to a smooth construction phase. The community development authority can be helpful in conveying the purpose of the project, and gaining support and commitment. A local partner, working with a PMC, can also interact with the community in developing a common understanding and sense of direction regarding the project, its purpose, and its progress.

Major disruption does take place around a project; it is better to manage change in a direct and constructive way, than to deny that it is going on or that it will happen. In one country, the government deliberately introduced a market economy by giving the population equity in a major copper project. A foundation was set up to ensure that the indigenous people would benefit from the project. Services were contracted only to natives: some provided trucking services, others a vegetable market. The infrastructural needs of the project were used as opportunities to introduce people to a market economy.

Whatever the development goals are, some ongoing management approach for dealing with the change that will surely result from the project needs to be decided upon and set up early on.

Managing Start-Up

The transition from construction to operation can also be difficult. It results in a sudden reduction in the number of jobs — on the order of a decrease from 11,000 to 500. Major changes in consumption patterns and life-style will have occurred during construction. Some locals will have begun to imitate Western life-styles (golf, bridge, sewing), but, in all probability, no foreigners will have gone "native." Access to high income will have been cut back when the construction phase has been completed.

Measures must be taken to coordinate this transition in the smoothest way possible. The project manager of a nickel operation in Indonesia developed a thoughtful transition strategy. Preference was given to local people who had worked on the construction to staff the operating facility. For those hired at higher wage levels, their contract provided that they would be returned to their places of hire, thereby assuring a systematic dispersal of the group from the area.

The construction workers' contracts were negotiated with the local Department of Manpower, and 10 percent of their wages were set aside as a savings plan. At the end of the assignment, they were given the proceeds of this fund to help them in relocating. Finally, secondary, or spin-off, employment opportunities or other projects absorbed many people. Many were employed by other macroprojects either in the same country, or in other developing countries. Any of these arrangements for start-up need to be planned early in the project.

Integrating Interests and Goals

As one can see, there are many stakeholders in the development of a macroproject: owners, project management contractors, local and foreign laborers and professionals, their families, surrounding communities, financiers, buyers of the output, government ministries, etc. One can see from the foregoing that the web of interactions among these participants is complex, with the project management contractor and the owners holding the bulk of the responsibility to resolve the numerous conflicts that invariably arise. A common vision and shared excitement and momentum are critical to diverting the various participants from preoccupation with their own discomfort to concentration on the tasks of the project.

There are so many aspects of a macroproject to consider, it is not surprising that many projects are characterized by marked imbalances in their organizational structure: ingenious financial and marketing arrangements combined with poor project management organization — or preoccupation with obtaining the best technology, yet with little attention to market demand issues. Until the project is fully operational it is impossible to determine the success of a given project. Certainly, effective coordination does not occur by happenstance. Participants need to establish a system for project control at the outset of the project. Only by measuring performance against a plan is it possible to determine if the project is on course.

Clearly the political issues surrounding a macroproject are complex and of great importance. Ultimately, however, it is the economic competitiveness of the completed plant that will define its success. To complete a project on schedule and within budget, real collaboration must be achieved. Thus, in the final analysis, it is sound organizational relations between hosts and multinational guests that provide the best hope for achieving national goals.

7
The Achievement of Quality Collaboration

Macroproject activity at the volume and dimension described in this book is a relatively new phenomenon — confirmed by the fact that only thirteen percent of all macroprojects in this survey have reached completion, and many are scheduled to come on-stream well into the 1980s. One might say that a 'macroproject industry' has emerged to accommodate the unprecedented growth — in giant steps — of the faster growing developing countries over the last decade. At times, the mid-1970s seemed to participants as if there were no rules of the game with respect to collaborating at the new and more complex level required to support stronger host initiatives on these enormous undertakings. Project participants' experiences in transnational and transcorporate collaboration might be described as still in the experimental stages. Nevertheless, much has been learned from the many new forms of collaboration that resulted.

Perhaps the only thing that can be said about the future, then, is that it will diverge significantly from the past. As host countries make further development advances, they will continue to build local skills and management capabilities, thereby becoming increasingly more focused and more sophisticated in their dealings with multinationals.

What has been learned to date probably will not be lost in any future rashes of experimentation, however. New variations in deal-making approaches are not likely to render the groundrules that have evolved over the last decade defunct, although they may need to be refined and adapted to changing economic and technological conditions. The most essential lesson learned to date is that of 'balance.' Balance seems to be more important than any other single factor in establishing a constructive relationship between hosts and their international partners and competitors: It appeared over and over again in the macroproject survey that the right balance of risks and rewards among host and multinational guests, as powers shift and change throughout the project lifetime, was key to achieving a successful outcome.

The remainder of this chapter summarizes the groundrules which have surfaced to date for transnational partnerships, identifies the principal guidelines for managing such a collaboration throughout the actual development of a project, and discusses the longer-term implications for macroproject development based on management techniques as they are understood today.

GROUNDRULES FOR TRANSNATIONAL PARTNERSHIPS

The continuously emerging, though often erratic, self-awareness of the developing countries has found expression in the major reworking of the groundrules on which development contracts were designed and written over the past decade. What was a turbulent national identity crisis within many host countries has given way to an increasing clarity in the way they are defining the terms and conditions under which they are willing to enter into collaborative arrangements with multinational partners. The groundrules that have gained clarity during the 1970s might indeed hold the key to achieving quality collaboration in the future.

Macroprojects require a collaboration that is, in fact, a complex interrelationship among sponsors, financiers, experts in various technological areas, the technology providers, and the civic and community groups who surround the project and have a stake in it. Transnational partnerships involved in resource development projects follow a specific pattern, namely:

- They are typically sponsored by a private corporation and/or parastatal organization
- They are likely to have private capital, in addition to public funds or grants which they might be eligible for
- The participants have something exclusive to contribute (i.e., a unique technology or expertise, or market access)
- Any technological gaps that are not covered by the partnership can be filled by contracting out part or all of

the engineering or construction work to internationally respected firms.

- Problems encountered can arise as much from errors in partner selection as from managerial difficulties in the development phase of the project.

In contrast, infrastructure projects follow a slightly different pattern, namely:

- They are typically government planned and sponsored
- They rely on public sources of capital for financing, for the most part
- Expertise exists among local public authorities in addition to that of local private engineering/construction companies
- Any technological gaps remaining after local responsibilities are assigned are filled by contracting to international project managers or other contractors or consortia
- When unpopular, these projects are likely to arouse enormous civic protests among the various stakeholders in the community at large.

The common groundrules that can be traced include the following:

1. Be willing and prepared to participate on a whole or partial basis as the project requires. There has been a clear shift away from equity to contractual commitments, except in those cases where high risks are present and/or where multinational support is needed. Even those companies that are accustomed to complete freedom with respect to equity share to be taken have been accepting lower equity or no equity in lieu of contractual promises of output. In contrast, when management capabilities are not forthcoming locally, host sponsors have been willing to turn the management of their development project over to foreign engineering/construction companies. The companies who are major participants have become such by being willing to participate on a whole or partial basis, as the need arises from project to project.

2. Be willing to consider creative options when selecting partners. Companies that have long competed aggres-

sively against each other in the international arena have found themselves as macroproject partners in Third World projects, entering into commitments to share capital resources, technology, and market opportunities. Companies in unrelated businesses have also been working closely together, while companies that never before ventured abroad are finding courage, and competence, in numbers. Consortia partners, whether two, or a score or more companies or organizations, often of several nationalities, appear to have based their decision to collaborate on one common feature: their desire to share risks.

3. Be alert to and organize specifically for the transition points that will occur during the development phase of the macroproject. The need to clearly negotiate long-term sale of output has forced greater attention to the structure and functioning of the operating company, the delivery facilities and what the economics of the plant might be. The need to define construction tasks among partners, in turn, has forced consideration of how to achieve a smooth transfer from design to construction and from construction to start-up at the outset of the project. The turnkey concept has forced a definition of what is required to install a fully operational plant at a fixed cost. The fixed-fee parameters of a consortium have forced consideration of maximizing trade-off opportunities early-on. Thus, beyond merely syndicating risk, consortia partnership has been found to provide the framework by which many often-overlooked pitfalls are anticipated.

4. Be careful to select only feasible projects to work on. When complexity, whether internal or external, is allowed to outstrip available management talent and project control processes, then trouble begins. Setting up the parameters of the project that fall within the participants' proven capability to control offers the greatest assurance of success. A high risk project does not necessarily merit an 'avoid' response. It can represent an occasion to bid high, or select other joint venture partners to share the risk, as well as to write innovative or protective contracts. Low-risk projects do not necessarily

merit a 'bid' response. The list of potential bidders might be long, the need to undercut in price and quality too intense and potentially damaging to one's reputation. There appears to be a threshold of competence.

GUIDELINES FOR MANAGING THE COLLABORATION

When initiating a macroproject, it is important to realize that such a project very well may be at the state-of-the-art level and that in fact there may be no guidelines, except the ones that the project organizers and partners create for themselves. Projects meriting such enormous investments should not hesitate to enlist the assistance of professionals in determining the most appropriate guidelines for that specific project. Sociologists, lawyers, accountants, programmers, anthropologists, management consultants, human resource managers, scientists, public relations specialists are among the professional groups that may have a contribution to make to setting up and structuring the macroproject organization for its development phase — design, construction, and start-up, in particular.

To highlight two essential components, it is important that any such organizational structure include a vehicle for auditing the excellence of the partnership and project, and a framework for ensuring that the responsible project leaders are accountable to the principal stakeholders.

Audit of Excellence

The various partners need to know that things are proceeding correctly. The project control system identifies the status of the project, including input and output and defines the tasks and which organizations or contractors are responsible for them. The project control system shows when something is going off track. In addition, it is also necessary to establish quality standards and verification systems to ensure that everything is on track and at the optimum quality level. Signals need to be set up that will indicate not only when and that things are slipping, but that things are going well. Excellence in performance needs to be defined in a way that it can be recognized and measured. Stakeholders might play a part in taking these measurements.

1. The power balance among partners should be continually
   audited. Do the host and multinational sponsors share the
   same goals and concept of progress over time?   When
   should the owners and project managers reorganize their
   chains of command from a centralized to a decentralized
   project control organization?   Are the community groups
   surrounding the project adequately prepared for site
   preparation, construction, start-up shifts and changes?

2. The project concept needs to be communicated from the
   top management down the line to the laborers on a
   continuing basis.   Is everyone working with the same
   priorities and time constraints in mind?

3. Feedback systems need to be installed with respect to
   both statistical as well as interpersonal data.   Are any
   ideas, shortcuts or innovations generated by the local
   laborers or professional engineering/construction staff
   being heard by the project leaders?

Accountability to Stakeholders

Some stakeholders are in support of the progress the project
will bring — these might include the contractors, suppliers, and local
government.   Other stakeholders are often resistant to change or
progress — these might include local community, indigenous laborers, customs officials, etc.   Devices can be incorporated into the
organization of the project that will foster understanding and
constructive communication among these various groups.

1. Financiers, owners, lenders and the project manager need
   to know the status of the project.   The project control
   system will statisfy their requirements.

2. The local government and community need to know the
   long-term impact of the project.   A community development authority can provide this information on an ongoing basis, as changes are occurring.   In turn, they can
   also make project leaders aware of the concerns of the
   community.   These concerns should be dealt with in a
   serious manner and satisfactorily resolved, as considerable
   costs have been incurred by sponsors who have engaged in
   long-term conflicts and disputes with these groups.

3. The project managers, engineers, construction workers, local manufacturers, etc. need to know what the project will do for them in terms of their professional career and/or business development. The importance of their doing their very best job on the macroproject must be conveyed. Evaluation of performance throughout the life of the project, as well as incentives and bonuses (whether financial or prestigeous), and guarantees of follow-on work or contracts are ways of providing the necessary motivation.

4. The host country as a nation needs to grow, evolve, and become more self-determined. Effective training and counterpart development programs, organized and directed by multinational guests, support this need to grow. As managerial know-how is transferred, multinationals will need to evolve new service packages to support the host at its higher competence levels.

5. The multinational participants as sponsors and suppliers seek access to raw material supply and outlets for their latest technology. Fair and open channels for negotiation of joint venture activities and bidding on goods and service jobs, as well as genuine collaboration and faithful honoring of contractual commitments, will prove to maximize the benefits for both sides.

LONG-TERM IMPLICATIONS

Future success depends upon the ability of OECD nations to adjust to the many changes that have occurred in the Third World over the last decade, and to make decisions, and determined commitments that will foster and nourish further growth in the developing nations over the decade to come.

For all of the experience which hosts and multinationals have accumulated during the 1970s, there are still many management questions that remain unanswered. Experiences to date are not being shared on an ongoing basis. Thus, insight and theory-building are not being promoted or encouraged at this time. New policies and further research are critical to facilitating further macroproject advancements — both within the Third World and throughout those global industries that macroproject development affects.

New Commitments to Global Development Needed

For all of the effort that went into post-oil-embargo development, the decade ended in a disappointing way. As many as 20 percent of the macroprojects launched during the 1970s are currently postponed or suspended: Some of the premier industrialization projects were underway in global project industry sectors suffering from severe over-capacity; some were underway in countries suffering from extraordinary political upheaval and even war; while remarkably few were designated irrevocably infeasible.

Financial problems have emerged. Capital had been borrowed extensively on the assumption that oil demand would be sustained and that consistently high (and even increasing) prices could be demanded for it. The oil-rich countries did not seem to share the wisdom (or skepticism) of the metal-rich sectors or government ministeries — that commodities are vulnerable to sweeping variations in demand and price and are not very responsive to the predictions of long-term forecasters.

In fact, there are forces at work which render forecasting almost impossible. The competitive dynamics that existed between developing and industrialized markets over the last decade suggest that the future will not be a smooth one. An essentially destructive antagonism appears to exist between industrialized and developing economies that underlies the difficulties and disappointments that both are experiencing at this time.

- OECD countries and their multinational oil companies have retaliated fiercely to the oil embargo and sudden pre-eminence of the Third World hydrocarbon processing industry by massively shifting exploration and investment to industrialized regions; aggressively pursuing new supply sources and substitute technologies (such as synfuels, coal and solar energy); and promoting greater consumer efficiencies, to reduce consumption of foreign oil. These initiatives were so intense that industrialized countries have managed to achieve a total production level slightly above that of developing countries, for the first time ever, in 1982. The result: global overcapacity, and plummeting profits for both sides.

- The metal resource development sector similarly could be a candidate for wholesale desertion in the foreseeable future. The remaining resources to be extracted are in inaccessible, and therefore costly, locations in the developing world. In contrast, meteorites containing mounds of rich minerals are whirling through space, and given moderate advances in space technology, and minor adaptations of the space shuttle concept, these could be mined by metal companies over the next one to two decades. Such extraction projects would need to be done in consortia, however, to adequately syndicate the risks. Any major antagonism could speed up investment in the necessary technological problem areas.

- At the same time, OECD countries continue to fiercely protect and falsely subsidize mature and inefficient industries (such as steel, textiles) — in spite of the fact that developing countries can produce the same output in newer and more efficient facilities that are close to the raw material sources with considerably more economical labor. The argument for their protectionism is that these are core components of their economies and cannot be surrendered.

These defensive postures will only foster an increasingly more protectionistic and closed world. If the development process really is to take its course, commitments need to be made by OECD and host nations alike, as well as by macroproject participants, both host and guest, to meet the macroproject requirements in increasingly more creative, constructive and flexible ways.

1. Capital sourcing could be improved and innovated. Financial vehicles will require substantial innovation over the next decade, as the high cost of short-term, bank-sponsored debt has driven many of the strongest and most creditworthy host countries to the brink of backrupcy. Direct barter and various formulae for countertrade will be experimented with by the more innovative multinational supporters of Third World growth. Besides extending more growth opportunities to developing countries, such approaches could provide important vehicles for growth for those Poor-I, Poor-II, and Poor-III countries who have been left behind.

2. <u>Technology could be transferred to Third World countries
    in more creative and integrated ways</u>. Both host govern-
    ments and their multinational consultants and advisors
    need to question the development process itself and
    wrestle more creatively with the optimum route to
    industrialization for their particular country. Up to this
    point, the notion of development has consisted of an
    evolutionary concept, namely, that developing economies
    follow in the footsteps of the more advanced countries in
    a sequential way. This has not been challenged by any
    developing country. Yet the world has seen that within
    technology groups or industry sectors the late-bloomer can
    frequently take a giant step over the technological level
    of the early innovators. An example is the relative
    inefficiency of the New York subway system as compared
    with the Paris or San Francisco systems. In fact, industry
    growth curves can be deliberately changed and influenced
    through product innovation and reposition. OPEC's oil
    embargo move had just such an effect in oil-exporting
    countries. Third World countries should consider not
    merely emulating, but developing a quite different strate-
    gy. There are countries, for example, who simply do not
    have the internal scale to sponsor a macroproject because
    of their small, local markets. Such countries, often with
    less than two million population, might continue to follow
    the industrialization road to development or they might
    consider a strategy of becoming a haven or paradise in an
    over-industrialized world. Perhaps they might choose to
    be a service center, or a hub of tourism.

    In addition, the technology that is transferred could
    be more responsive to the local setting. It is not
    uncommon to find public facilities and housing projects in
    Third World cities that are callous and cold, low-cost
    construction. A marked rupture exists between the charm
    of the countryside, regardless of how primitive, and the
    newly mushrooming cities built on a tight budget. The
    recent rennovations of major U.S. cities confirms that
    architects and designers are finally learning how to make
    city centers livable and pleasing. A synthesis might be

achieved between 'architectural lines' and the 'bottom line' to bring architectural breakthroughs within the reach of Third World budgets.

3. The theory of open and competitive markets for goods and services needs to be followed by all players in all industry sectors, if the development process is really going to become a possibility for all countries. A first step might be for multinationals to seriously consider surrendering their mature and struggling industries such as steel and textiles to Third World production. Such transfers of key industries would require that the nations involved be fairly comfortable that the world will be a secure and peaceful one, however. On the other hand, it is believed by many that such moves toward heightened global interdependence are the only ways to really ensure peace.

The key to avoiding the violent swings experienced during the 1970s is, again, "balance." In the case of oil, if prices had been raised only to a threshold point below that making other energy sources or exploration sites suddenly economically feasible, the intense competition experienced would not have resulted. In contrast, the more close-knit partnerships in the metal sector foster a close collaboration in a very turbulent business. The most critical future pursuit will be that of identifying and defining the middle ground — and negotiating a deal accordingly.

Further Advances in Project Management Required

Whether management expertise has been developed to a level of competence adequate enough to meet the requirements of future projects remains the critical question. Although there are major corporate organization structures that are enormous in scale and span the globe, their management systems and approaches have been developed to bureaucratize repetition and routine. A macroproject has more in common with military management during wartime than with corporate life at a multinational's headquarters. It is organized to achieve specific objectives within a limited and clearly defined timeframe at a predetermined cost. Each work package is performed only once (hopefully). Because the task was never done previously at the specific location, numerous "surprise attacks" — whether geological, environmental, etc. — are common.

The only way that participants can develop a competence in macroproject management is to take responsibility for as many macroprojects as possible under as many varying circumstances and in as many diverse locations as possible.

Regardless of how many errors are made, or how many difficulties are encountered, when it is completed a macroproject achievement speaks for itself. When the first phase of the King Abdulaziz International Airport opens in Saudi Arabia in 1985, more than 10,000 workers will have been involved in the construction and $4.3 billion will have been paid for the goods and services that went into it. A self-contained city, including a desalination plant, hospital, and telephone system, it will have the capacity to absorb 15,000 to 20,000 permanent employees, and manage 100 flight operations per hour and 8.6 million passengers per year by 1985. As the largest airport construction project in the world, all of the complexities of construction will seem inconsequential when compared with the awesomeness of the achievement.

As large as the Saudi project is, it is dwarfed when compared with some future dreams. Scientists envision that the largest planned project in the aerospace industry will be a manned space platform facility to conduct scientific research, astronomical observation, and earth watch, as well as to provide energy and material resources and strategic stability. Such a project will cost $6.8 to $46.2 billion over 8 to 17 years, or $1.5 to $4.5 billion per year. By comparison, the largest macroproject in the Third World sample is $21 billion and will take 20 years to build.

As the space program moves to a point of serious implementation of these manned space stations, it will become clear that that project has many things in common with macroprojects in the Third World, namely, a) people and politics will be equivalent in importance with physics and science as the key variables to be managed; b) logistics will be difficult due to the remote location, and the long lead times in receiving goods ordered; c) the cultural ruptures involved in uprooting large numbers of people will have to be managed by the project leaders; and d) the scale will be massive, among the largest known to date.

The prognosis for conducting such a project successfully is mixed.

- Technically, it has been proven that projects of enormous scale can be launched. Massive resources can be brought to bear on a project. Risk and exposure of individual participants can be reduced to tolerable levels via syndication. Enormous manpower resources can be transported to remote locations, and the very best organizations from around the world can be marshalled for a particular task.

- Humanity may stunt progress, however, as problems in collaborating in a smooth way at the world-scale level stubbornly persist. Further, it still seems a chronic occurrence that important environmental, social and political issues go unnoticed and unanticipated, causing backfires at the most inappropriate times — ultimately creating costly budget overruns and schedule violations.

Major innovations in negotiation and conflict resolution capabilities and project management systems remain to be realized. Further study is needed. In-depth reexamination of the major macroprojects accomplished during the 1970s would provide invaluable hindsite, as well as supporting material for the development of the breakthrough notions and concepts so critical to realizing future goals.

Macroprojects are surfacing problems and inadequacies that are at the forefront of technological and management thinking and debate. At this time, it is really not within the scope of current expertise to realize man's loftiest dreams in a completely painless way. Nevertheless, both host and multinational participants are actively engaged in advancing this expertise with each increasingly more complex and more difficult project they conceive of and manage to bring to fruition.

> "...the true human successes are those which triumph over the mysteries of matter and of life. At that moment a decisive hour will sound for mankind, when the spirit of discovery absorbs all the momentum contained in the spirit of war."
> —Teilhard de Chardin

Index

186